THE BUILDINGS OF BRADFORD

ST. GEORGE'S HALL

THE BUILDINGS OF BRADFORD

AN ILLUSTRATED ARCHITECTURAL HISTORY

GEORGE SHEERAN

TEMPUS

For John Ayers, who did this first

Frontispiece: St George's Hall

First published 2005

Tempus Publishing Limited
The Mill, Brimscombe Port,
Stroud, Gloucestershire, GL5 2QG
www.tempus-publishing.com

British Library Cataloguing in Publication Data.
A catalogue record for this book is available from the British Library.

ISBN 0 7524 3584 1

Typesetting and origination by Tempus Publishing Limited.
Printed in Great Britain.

CONTENTS

PREFACE AND ACKNOWLEDGEMENTS

When I was invited to write this history of Bradford's buildings, I didn't realise the task I was about to undertake. It wasn't the subject itself, complicated as this was. Years of research and teaching at the University of Bradford on courses about the history of architecture and urban development had given me a thorough grounding in the subject. The problem was – is – that Bradford is undergoing a widespread regeneration of its urban environment with buildings of the twentieth century being demolished and earlier, often neglected, buildings being restored. What I had photographed one week was demolished the next; what I had commented on as a pitifully derelict Victorian building was soon to become sheathed in scaffolding and to undergo a transformation. As I write, the 1960s centre of Bradford is being cleared and reconstructed. Under these circumstances I make no apologies for buildings or areas of the city that I have portrayed in a poor light, for some may have been brought back to life after going to press; rather I feel a sense of bemusement, as many Bradfordians may at the present time. Let us hope that this momentum for regeneration is sustained and has a successful outcome.

This study is the product of reading, discussions and observation over a number of years. But more specifically I should like to thank the following people: the staffs of both Bradford Central Library's Local Studies department and West Yorkshire Archive Service, Bradford, who have all helped me in identifying the dates and architects of buildings. I am also grateful to my wife, Yanina Sheeran, and my colleague Paul Jennings who read through early drafts, and whose comments have saved me from several pitfalls. I should also like to thank Geoff Layer, Dean of the School of Lifelong Education and Development, for making time available for the completion of this book.

George Sheeran
March, 2005

1 BRADFORD: A CITY DEFINED

Bradford: Place and Space

Bradford is a stone city. It doesn't nestle at the foot of the Pennines, but climbs up hills and sprawls along valleys in an urban conglomeration of buildings mostly of the nineteenth and twentieth centuries. Roads descend into its centre, while to the north road, rail and canal snake along the Aire Valley leading to Skipton. The underlying geology of Bradford is dominated by carboniferous sandstones of great variety and quality from rough rock to fine, hard, honey-coloured building stones. There are thick, heavy flags used much in paving; thinly bedded sandstones that split into 'slates' for roof coverings; there are hard-wearing sets; stone that can be cut into troughings, spoutings and gullies to convey water; stones that can be piled up into mill chimneys or sculpted into the angels that watch silently over the dead in Bradford's cemeteries. Try as they might, architects of the 1960s and '70s and no end of tower blocks in glass, concrete or Portland stone were ever quite able to subdue this sandstone heritage.

Yet Bradford is as much an imagined place as a real one, constructed in the images handed to us by writers and others. It is a grim-faced Industrial Revolution city whose economy was based on wool, and where canny Yorkshiremen made quick fortunes. 'Where there's muck, there's brass', 'rags to riches', 'Millionaire's Row' – all these phrases seem to have been made-to-measure for the nineteenth-century city. Even T.S. Eliot could raid this store of images when he portrayed one of his characters in 'The Waste Land' as 'One of the low on whom assurance sits/ As a silk hat on a Bradford millionaire'. The canny purse-proud Bradford of the popular imagination was probably only ever that; and it is significant that such imaginings arise only from the nineteenth-century city, not the eighteenth, while in the twentieth century Bradford's image underwent a change and hardened into something more aggressive. By the late 1970s and '80s it had become identified with the city's contender for the world heavyweight boxing championship, Richard Dunn. It also became identified with the dark side of human nature in murderers who achieved an infamy of national proportions – Donald Neilson or Peter Sutcliffe, the Yorkshire Ripper. Now a different sort of perception also came into focus – Bradford was also a place of high immigration, of declining industry and urban degeneration; Bradford as a place of riot, racial tensions and social dislocation. Bradford was a 'newsy' city, as one advertisement for a job in the media put it. While it is easy to find examples to back these perceptions, this is a far cry from Bradford as a city and other places within the borders of the Bradford Metropolitan District. To the north, towns along the Aire Valley and especially within Wharfedale contain well-heeled and somewhat exclusive areas around Ilkley or Menston, towns that were little-touched by the heavy industrialisation of the nineteenth century and which retain a country air. There are exceptions: some towns in the Aire Valley such as Keighley do not fit this image, having been former centres of industry. But these and other places within the Metropolitan District all grew and developed because of Bradford's influence in the nineteenth and early twentieth centuries, were coupled by economic links to the city's fortunes, and also by its entrepreneurial and professional classes who desired rural retreats. Pleas for secession from the Metropolitan District are more common today, although perhaps a disassociation from the image more than the political control of Bradford is as strong a factor here.

This raises a further issue, one of space and boundary. Looking at Bradford from an historical perspective, it is possible to define at least five boundaries: the parish, which was large and included such places as Shipley and Haworth several miles to the north and west; the town, which was equivalent to what we would today think of as the main shopping streets in the city centre; the municipal borough, which was founded in 1847 and comprised Bradford, Bowling, Great Horton, Little Horton and Manningham; the city, which came into being in 1897 and covered an extended borough boundary to include a number of towns and villages on its perimeter; and the Bradford Metropolitan District, which was formed in 1974 and is by far the largest of these administrative units, taking in parts of the Aire and Wharfe Valleys. In order to keep this study to an appropriate size, neither the largest nor the smallest of these areas will be used, but the historic borough formed in 1847. This is an area that had both an historic unity and identity, and it was also the area in which much of Bradford's industrialisation took place in the nineteenth century. Today the old borough retains much of this identity in terms of its heritage of building and its character as a built environment generally. This will not be followed in slavish conformity to the boundary, rather it is indicative of the area of study, and where developments in the borough had prompted related or directly connected developments just outside, then it is sensible to pursue these. As Asa Briggs observed in *Victorian Cities* in 1963 when writing about the industrial village of Saltaire founded by the Bradford industrialist Titus Salt three miles to the north of Bradford at Shipley, 'there could have been no Saltaire had there not been first a Bradford.'[1]

The great nineteenth-century city had grown from humble beginnings. City status was acquired relatively late – Bradford was no ancient city. But in this respect Bradford was hardly exceptional, since Leeds and Sheffield were granted city status in the late nineteenth century also. Where Bradford was different was in its size and relative importance, for while the industrial and population growth of the town was about to rocket at the beginning of the nineteenth century, Leeds was already the fifth largest provincial town in England and Wales by 1801, and the largest in Yorkshire; Sheffield was not far behind. To put some figures on this – the population of the *town* of Bradford in 1801 was 6,393; Keighley, in the Aire Valley to the north-west, was almost as big with a population of 5,745. Bradford's industrial neighbours were larger – Halifax, 8,866 and Huddersfield, 7,268. Bradford was also smaller than several of the industrial towns just across the Pennines in Lancashire. Yet Bradford was to outstrip them all in the course of the next sixty or seventy years.

What caused this growth is difficult to determine exactly (and will be more fully discussed in the next section). Bradford's geographical position should have hindered growth rather than stimulated it. As mentioned at the beginning of the chapter, the town stands at the foot of the Pennines within a bowl of hills, and until the eighteenth century had poor communications with the other parts of the county and across the Pennines. The spatial configuration of what was to become the borough of Bradford was made up of Bradford and its parish church and three out-townships – Manningham to the north, Bowling, and Great Horton and Little Horton around the southern perimeter. These places were villages and physically separated from Bradford by countryside, but connected to it by roads (figure 1a). These out-townships are all located on higher ground above Bradford. For many centuries two things tied them to Bradford: its market and its parish church, the out-townships possessing neither. Bradford was the market centre for the marketing of goods at its fairs and markets and provided the only place of worship. Things did not begin to change in this respect until the beginning of the eighteenth century.

This dependence on Bradford by its out-townships had almost certainly been established in the Middle Ages – Bradford's market charter dates from 1251, and the parish church (the present-day cathedral) dates from the Middle Ages also. But what had begun to change things by the eighteenth and nineteenth centuries was the growth of nonconformity. Nonconformity meant that there was less reliance on Bradford for religious provision, since nonconformist chapels and meeting rooms could be built in or near out-townships. Also, industrial growth led to a physical growth in the built environment along the main routes out of the town (figure 1b). Tentacular expansion along routes out of Bradford began to reduce the open space between Bradford and places like the Hortons and Bowling; Manningham was rather slower in this respect. But too much should not be made of this growth, since,

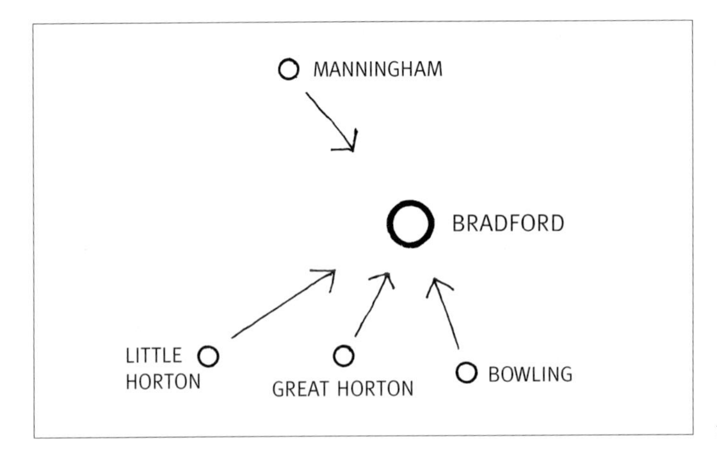

1a Before 1700

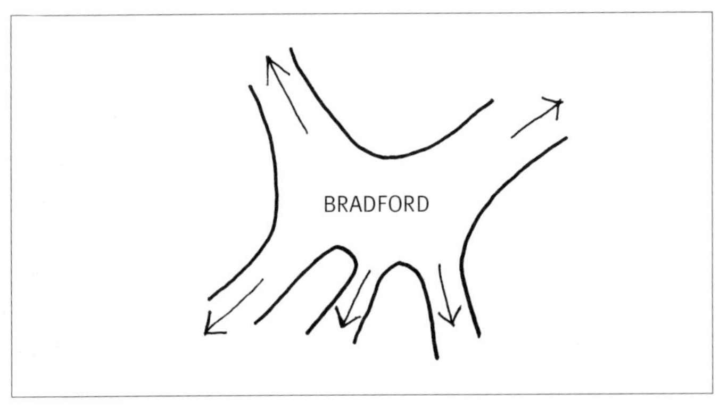

1b 1880-1850

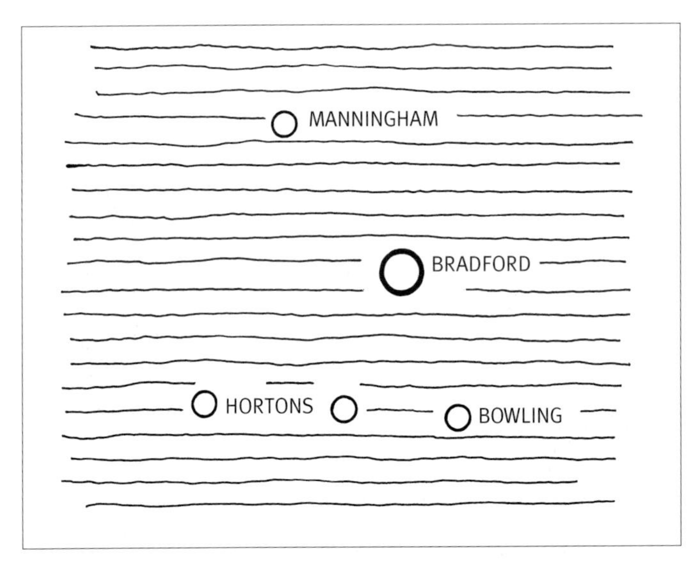

1c 1850-1900

Figure 1 The urban development of Bradford.

despite heavy population increases, it was not until the second half of the nineteenth century that town and out-townships became melded together as one urban area with little discontinuity (figure 1c).

By the second half of the nineteenth century, also, it is possible to interpret this development in terms of an emerging pattern. Returning to medieval Bradford – before the fifteenth century a pattern of streets had been established that was centred on the marketplace. These were streets that we would recognise today in terms of name and approximate alignment – Ivegate, Kirkgate and Westgate; Kirkgate led to the church. There was probably a further road, Silsbridge Lane, running in a westerly direction which was approximately on the site of the present-day Grattan Road (figure 2). While there were undoubtedly side roads and back lanes, the above were the principal streets and they were at the commercial and religious heart of this small town. It was a pattern that was to remain the same, and it was around these same streets that the town's commerce revolved, in fact they are still important areas. What changed in the nineteenth century was the scale of things as further streets devoted to trade and commerce were added and the centre of the old town became enmeshed in the growth of the new borough, although never completely lost. By 1870 or so what people had traditionally thought of as Bradford had become a central business district, while around it suburbs and industrial districts were arising. To the north, Manningham had become the borough's finest middle-class suburb, with a similar and slightly earlier one on the edge of the central business district and just to the west at Little Horton. Industry and large numbers

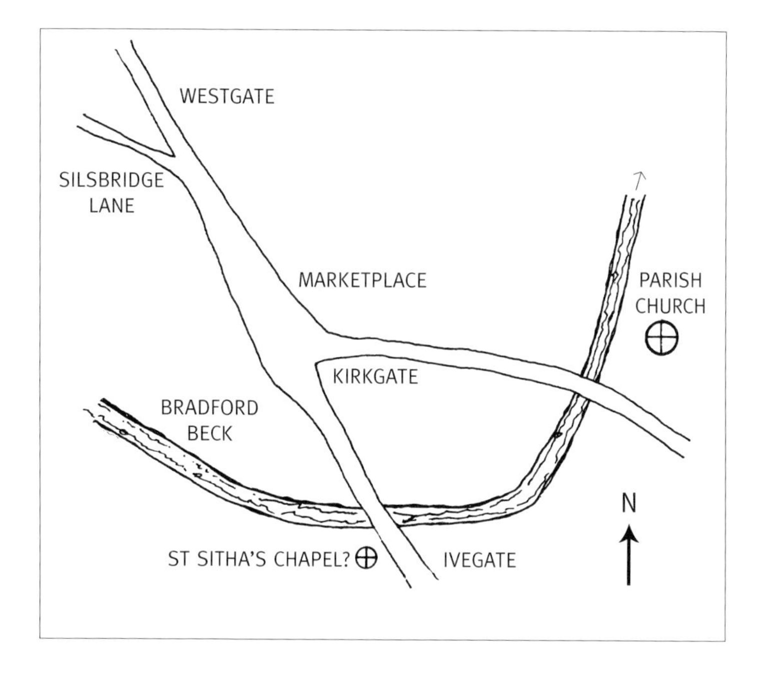

2 Conjectural plan of medieval Bradford.

of working-class houses built to the south of the centre halted the further expansion of the Little Horton suburb. The siting of these suburbs to the north and west was an important factor in their success, since prevailing westerly winds carried smoke away from the houses. Interesting in this respect was an attempt to build better-class houses to the east of the town on the valley side at Undercliffe. Hillside Villas, as the development became known, never progressed beyond a few houses and became hemmed-in by many streets of back-to-back terraces by the later nineteenth century. Perhaps smoke pollution was a factor in their failure. Of the other out-townships, Great Horton and Bowling saw similar increases, but in working-class housing and industry. These developments are represented in figure 3 in diagrammatic form. Admittedly this is something of an oversimplification – pockets of working-class housing and even industry could be found in or near to middle-class districts but, broadly speaking, it is correct.

What this pattern represents is the exodus of the middle class from the centre of the town. Exodus is probably too strong a word, since from the beginnings of Bradford's industrial and commercial growth in the nineteenth century middle-class families moving into the town had sought the shelter of developing suburbs. But some early entrepreneurial families such as the Rands or Garnetts and some clerical and professional families did leave the centre, although most worked there. The process can be projected forward also. Today many of Bradford's middle class have relocated away from the suburbs of the old borough, moving farther out still. While there had been a move to the north towards Heaton in the later nineteenth century, by the twentieth century places such as Shipley and towns along the Aire and Wharfe

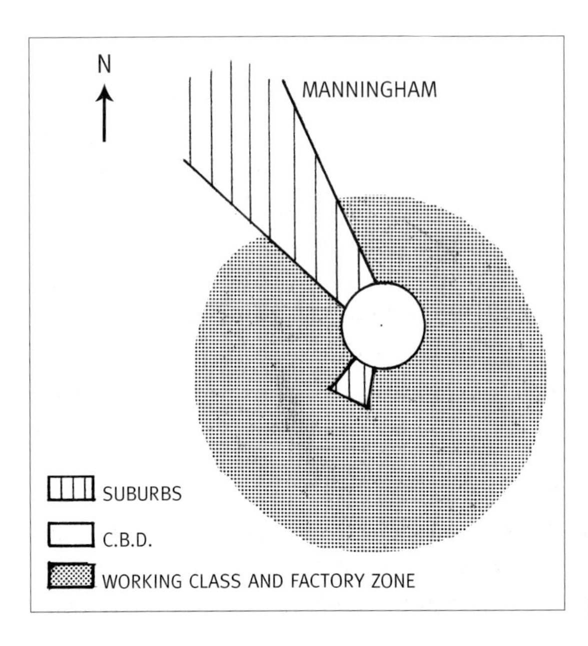

3 Social and economic divisions by 1870.

Valleys had become residential areas while the old suburbs such as Manningham had become redefined as the inner city – 'white flight' is the rather dramatic phrase that some use to describe this population movement. However, a cooler assessment must take into account that people have been leaving the inner city areas of Bradford since the 1920s, especially for places on the edges of the borough where either council or privately built estates were being located. Nevertheless, while the proportion of the South Asian population of Bradford is about 18-20% for the Metropolitan District as a whole, its distribution is uneven and is concentrated heavily within the old borough where South Asian families, and especially Pakistani families, make up 30-50% of the population of some wards. It is senseless to suggest that racial tensions do not exist in these areas, and Manningham in particular has become the location of several serious incidents over the years, with rioting in the summer of 2001.

Despite this, central Bradford continues as a major place of employment within the district. If traditional industries have declined, shops, offices and the service industries draw a constant stream of commuter traffic into the centre. Two sectors have grown enormously since their beginnings in the nineteenth century: local government and education. A university is probably one of the markers of a city in the late twentieth and early twenty-first centuries, and Bradford has a well-developed further and higher education quarter just near the centre of the city at the foot of Great Horton Road. It consists of the university and a large college of further education that stand side-by-side. The growth of such 'Latin quarters' is one of the most significant additions to the built environments of cities in the past century, and Bradford is no exception.

A City's Past

While admitting that there was little evidence of early settlement on the site of Bradford, nineteenth-century local historians spent quite a lot of effort in trying to find it. 'It is very probable that a Brigantian town stood on the site of Bradford', wrote John James[2] in 1841. The post-Conquest period provided him with richer pickings: Bradford was associated with medieval military leaders, and the mention of a manor house in a medieval document was in his narrative turned into the site of a castle[3]. The truth is that the early history of Bradford is obscure. The project that historians such as James were engaged in was providing the new factory town of the mid-nineteenth century with a lineage, a past lost in Celtic mists and associated with knights and castles of the Middle Ages. Bradford, of course, had a past, but the perspective from which we might view it today is that of trying to discover the life and organisation of a small medieval town.

Here we hit a problem: could Bradford be considered a town as long ago as the thirteenth, fourteenth or even the fifteenth century? Some of the characteristics of a town are diversified occupations and trades, rather than wholly agricultural occupations, markets, and perhaps municipal forms of administration. None of the out-townships had such characteristics, and Bowling, Great and Little Horton and Manningham should be regarded as villages presided over by the lord of the manor or his steward at the court baron, the manor court. Bradford had a market that was chartered in 1251, and it also had a fair. We also know from medieval documents such as surveys, taxation records and court documents that there were a number of different trades in Bradford, and that there were burgesses. This last group of people is important. A burgess was a person who held property by burgage tenure – that is a rent that was paid to free the holder from agricultural services to the lord of the manor – which left him free to pursue a trade. The problem, as far as Bradford is concerned, is that no form of town government accompanied this – no council, or borough court; no surviving charter that conferred such rights, as there was at Leeds, say. All the business of the town seems to have been conducted in the lord of the manor's court baron. Court rolls do survive for parts of the fourteenth and fifteenth centuries, and from these and other documents we can glean something of Bradford's past.[4] Set down are such things as Bradford's early street names – Ivegate, Kirkgate and Westgate (old Norse: *gata*, a way or lane); that there were permanent stalls in the marketplace in Westgate which could be rented at the court baron; and that the burgesses paid their rent into the court.

By the late Middle Ages the principal commercial area of the town seems to have been along and at the junction of these streets. Here there were shops, market stalls and places to eat and drink. There were also butchers within the town who had erected a shambles, and their presence suggests a ready market for meat and the cattle that would have to be slaughtered there. The court rolls give us an insight into how widespread the influence of even a small place like Bradford might be. In 1411 an inquiry of the court had established that beasts brought to the market at Bradford were depasturing local grazing. The sellers of cattle came from within the immediate neighbourhood of Bradford, Liversedge for instance, but they also came from farther afield, north along the Aire Valley – Bingley and Bradley – and even farther – Broughton, Gisburn and Craven. However the court rolls tell us more than this. Much has been made by earlier historians of two crafts practised in Bradford: shoe-making and textile production. Throughout the rolls shoemakers are mentioned, as are occupations such as weaver and dyer together with references to a fulling mill (for cleansing and thickening woollen cloth). Neither trade should surprise us, for the histories of most medieval English towns reveal the same or similar occupations: footwear and clothing were needed everywhere. In other words, the local needs to be placed within a national context. However, we should note one genuinely local or regional development: the shift of a clothing industry based on the production of woollen cloth for export from traditional centres in the east of the county around Beverley and York, to the west. This development seems to have been taking place from the later fifteenth and into the sixteenth century. It is perhaps from the latter date that wool textile manufacture in the Bradford area reached levels of production greater than that of purely local consumption.

There were other trades and industries as well, especially if we look outside the immediate centre of Bradford. Again from the court rolls we know that there was ironmaking. Several references occur, such as the agreement made in 1411 between the lord of the manor and Thomas Thorne allowing the latter to carry 'Urestone' (iron ore) across Bradford Moor. There are also scattered references to lime kilns, quarries and coal pits. While this may have been small scale, it nevertheless indicates that the Bradford region had a diversified economy by the fifteenth century, and not one based solely on agriculture.

A further important role that the town of Bradford played was in religious provision. The parish of Bradford covered a wide area, as already noted. Although there may have been one or two private chapels in wealthy households at Bowling or Horton, it was St Peter's, the parish church standing at the end of Kirkgate, that provided a place of worship for the majority of the people in the parish, although there was a chapel at Haworth, some ten miles away and built there for obvious reasons of distance. There must have been some pressure on the clergy to provide masses on a Sunday for the population of the whole of this parish, and this is perhaps one of the reasons for the building of a further chapel within the town. This chapel, dedicated to St Sitha, is mentioned in two sources: John Leyland, Henry VIII's antiquary, mentioned it when he passed through the town around 1544; but there is an earlier reference to the chapel of the Holy Trinity and St Sitha that occurs in the register of George Neville, archbishop of York, in 1466. Bridge chapels, either at the ends of or on bridges, were common in medieval England. Such chapels provided extra space for services, and were perhaps a reminder to travellers to give thanks or to pray for safety when undertaking a journey as they passed over a bridge in or out of town – as this statement in the archbishop's register suggests:

> To our beloved inhabitants of the town of Bradford in our diocese; in as much as a chapel in honour of the Holy Trinity and St Sitha, the virgin, has been erected, situated at the end of the bridge at Bradford aforesaid, the present license shall enable any suitable chaplains to celebrate masses and other divine offices ... so that to you and all travellers coming thither to hear such chaplains as may be permitted to celebrate ... according to the tenor of this present granted faculty, and special license during our good pleasure ...[5]

Does this imply that the chapel had only recently been built?

By the fifteenth century Bradford possessed some urban characteristics in its variety of trades, numbers of burgesses and regular markets. People from the surrounding district brought their produce and their beasts to market at Bradford, and would have been themselves able to buy goods and services and no doubt enjoy the hospitality of alehouses. Yet Bradford is perhaps best regarded as a market centre rather than a town, for it was at the centre of an agricultural community, and if there were shops along Kirkgate there were also barns; not far from the marketplace were common fields, and the settlements of Bowling, Great and Little Horton and Manningham were reliant on Bradford and were villages with mostly agricultural economies and occupations.

The majority of the population of this district were probably farmers and labourers. In the centre of Bradford around the marketplace is where we would expect to find a sprinkling of burgesses and traders; there were also probably numbers of craftsmen who may also have possessed small agricultural holdings. But there were also two smaller groupings of people not mentioned so far. Firstly gentry families who made their livings through their rent rolls of tenants and who had established one or two good houses in the district – Bolling Hall, for example – and probably a manor house in Great Horton. Secondly there was the clergy who, as literate religious leaders within a large parish, probably wielded a good deal of influence.

Medieval Bradford has been discussed in some detail, because the Middle Ages were one of two significant periods of urbanisation, the other being the nineteenth century. While Bradford as an urban environment undoubtedly changed in the seventeenth and eighteenth centuries, it was during the previous centuries that its plan had become established and the locations of significant public buildings and spaces for trade had been brought into being. This was a plan that was not altered substantially until the nineteenth century. Ivegate, Kirkgate and Westgate remained the principal streets and converged on the marketplace. Within the marketplace the junction of Kirkgate and Westgate was known as Pycorner – not, perhaps, because pies were sold there, but because it may have been the site of the court of piepoudre. 'Pie Powder', as the term became known in English, was the court in which disputes at markets and fairs were settled. This may have been housed in the toll booth situated at the same junction, which was probably a multi-functional building where market tolls were taken and where the courts of pie powder and the courts baron of the manor were held, functions that were retained in part until the nineteenth century. This was as much civic administration as Bradford seems to have possessed and although we know something about it, we have to guess at a good deal – even the buildings have disappeared.[6]

One thing, however, was to change quite a lot in the course of the sixteenth and seventeenth centuries and that was religion and religious observance. While the parish church remained, of course, it became Anglican under the reforms of Henry VIII, but further repercussions followed. It seems likely that St Sitha's Chapel was removed in the reform of chapels and chantries carried out under Edward VI. Although the accounts of Edward's commissioners do not survive in their entirety, we do know that they were active in Bradford parish because they allowed the chapel at Haworth[7] to continue because of distance, but there is no mention of St Sitha's after the sixteenth century. Apart from the disappearance of this chapel, little else seems to have occurred that would have had a marked effect on the urban environment of Bradford. However, Protestantism was established in the town and by the end of the next century nonconformist faiths and the numbers of people practising them had grown.

4 A nineteenth-century engraving of the junction of Ivegate and Westgate. At this junction was the marketplace (just visible to the extreme left); the tall building in the background stands on the site of the old toll booth at Pycorner and may well have contained medieval work. The house shown in the middle is in several occupations, with retail premises at ground level and below ground. It probably represents the remodelling of a building of medieval origins. This entire site was redeveloped in the nineteenth century.

From the early years of the eighteenth century numbers of houses and other premises had been licensed for services and preaching, and by the latter half of the century all of the major nonconformist faiths had erected chapels around the perimeter of Bradford – Baptists, Congregationalists, Quakers and Unitarians all possessed places of worship. In 1776 the Wesleyan Methodists had erected the Octagon Chapel in Great Horton Road not far from the site of the present Alhambra Theatre in the centre of Bradford. This phenomenon was arguably the most significant to have occurred in Bradford during the seventeenth and eighteenth centuries, because the buildings mentioned not only extended the urban fabric, but also represented long-run changes of attitude and religious belief which spanned generations and challenged the supremacy of the Anglican Church.

Others might argue that the rise of the clothing industry – the manufacture of wool textiles – was equally, if not more, important. The position of Bradford with regard to woollen cloth production in the Middle Ages has been discussed above.

Undoubtedly cloth was made here in the Middle Ages, but one must be careful about making connections between this and the huge economic success of the nineteenth century. Little is known about the extent of Bradford's medieval industry, although some historians in the nineteenth century tried to make much of it. The essential thing to hold on to is the relocation of the industry as mentioned already – from the east of the county around Beverley, York and other towns to the West Riding. If wool textiles were being produced in the Bradford district during the sixteenth and seventeenth centuries, what types were these? According to Fieldhouse[8], Bradford thrived on 'Turkey work', that is, a heavy, patterned woollen cloth used for upholstery; he suggests that lack of demand for this sort of material in the second half of the seventeenth century had led to a crisis in the local industry, which may have died out. On the other hand, we know from a taxation dispute that earlier in the century woollen cloth was being produced in abundance. John Dixon of Shipley (three miles to the north of Bradford) had testified in 1638 that:

> In the Towne of Shipley ... and the Townes adionynge there are now about an hundred Clothiers for one that then [forty years previously] were in those Townes.[9]

The cloth woven appears to have been kerseys, a kind of course, long, narrow cloth. Perhaps the position was that kerseys continued in production while Turkey work ceased. Certainly by the beginning of the eighteenth century Bradford could be regarded as part of an expanding region of wool textile production at the heart of the West Riding, a region often referred to as the clothing district and approximately equivalent to the present West Yorkshire conurbation.

'Wool textiles' is a carefully chosen term, for the types of cloth made fall into the two broad categories of woollens and worsteds. Woollens were made from short staple (short fibre) wools, their strength being derived as much from the tendency of the fibres to tangle together as from the warp and weft. Worsteds are produced from a long staple wool that is combed straight before being spun and twisted to produce a strong yarn. Worsteds, because they could be manufactured with a fine strong finish, were suitable for a variety of goods to which woollens were not suited – linings for example or fine coverlets.

The great seats of trade in wool textiles within the clothing districts lay around the towns of Halifax, Huddersfield, Leeds and Wakefield – but not Bradford. All of these, except Bradford, had cloth or piece halls by the beginning of the eighteenth century where textile goods could be bought or commissioned by merchants. Bradford's trade in textiles is more difficult to gauge. Merchants from these surrounding towns did visit Bradford to buy cloth, and there were one or two merchants and woolstaplers (dealers in raw wool) with residences in Bradford, but much of the business that was carried on seems to have been conducted at inns within the central town. When a piece hall was built in Bradford for the first time in 1773, it was small and did not match the magnificent classical designs of piece halls elsewhere in the county such as at Halifax or Leeds. It was demolished in the nineteenth century, but sketches show that it had a vernacular quality. It had stalls for 100 clothiers and in 1780 was enlarged to accommodate a further 150 stalls. This seems large at first, but is a telling figure when compared with Leeds, say, where the Coloured Cloth Hall of 1756 contained over 1,700 stalls; the White Cloth Hall, rebuilt in 1776, contained above 1,200 stalls. On the scale of eighteenth-century cloth halls, Bradford's came near to the bottom. However, what needs to be emphasised here is the scale of things, for in other respects Bradford had some essentials in common with the other textile towns – its position as the centre of marketing for a textile-based hinterland, for instance. While some cloth was almost certainly manufactured in Bradford itself, the bulk of production was located in the out-townships and villages over a wider area. Much of this cloth was sold in the Bradford market as records of stallholders at the Piece Hall indicate, although other clothiers in the Bradford district also sold their cloth in both the Leeds and the Halifax markets. This suggests two things: firstly that Bradford township was a centre of marketing rather than production; secondly that Bradford in the eighteenth century played a part, but a relatively small part, in the region's textile trade, despite the fact that textiles may have been a major occupation. A further point needs to be made in passing, but which will be discussed in detail later. Although we associate Bradford with wool textiles, Great and Little Horton had a flourishing calico industry that was of some importance to these townships until financial reverses in banking and commerce brought it to an end in the mid-nineteenth century. The point being that Bradford's textile base was already diversified to some extent.

Endeavour in textiles brought with it distinctive forms of architecture, although a good deal of this early building has been lost to the district. The Piece Hall in Kirkgate and the fulling mills, where woollen cloth was cleansed and then dried on tenter frames, were cleared away in the nineteenth century. The most distinctive forms of architectural expression, however, were the cottages and houses of textile workers or clothiers. These usually consisted of living accommodation together with loomshops or comb shops and possibly a small warehouse, but few in the Bradford district now survive from this early period. The reason for this is again demolitions and clearances in the nineteenth and also in the twentieth century.

The cause of much of this razing of earlier property was a huge growth in the nineteenth century, and while the establishment of a textile industry was important, so too was Bradford's geographical position. If it was difficult to access by road, it had other advantages: its smallness and semi-rural character. As already discussed above, in 1801 it was scarcely larger than a rural industrial town like Keighley in the Aire Valley, and it was smaller than its other commercial neighbours. This gave Bradford a capacity for expansion. There were other factors too – a tradition of labour organisation within the textile industry and large deposits of coal and ironstone in some parts of the district. All of this was to lead to a rapid industrialisation of Bradford and the swallowing-up of the earlier towns and traditional ways of life by the hungry new factory town.

To understand this massive growth of industry and population in nineteenth-century Bradford, it is necessary to take stock of the scene in 1780 or 1790, for this is where the origins of Bradford's industrial revolution lie. By 1790 little in the way of mechanisation in the industry other than in the carding and spinning processes had occurred, and this aided the domestic industry. The organisation of the trade was probably more important, with merchants or master manufacturers putting out spinning or weaving sometimes over a wide area and collecting in the finished products for sale. This practice was well established in the worsted industry. But looking beyond textiles, two ironworks of great importance to Bradford had been brought into being by 1800: Bowling Ironworks around 1788 and, just outside the old borough to the south, Low Moor Ironworks around 1791. Then in 1798 a syndicate of businessmen – Swaine, Ramsbothom and Murgatroyd – began the first mill in Bradford, which was operational by 1800. The Holme Mill, as it was known, has acquired iconic status for local historians as the first wool textile mill in Bradford to be powered by steam. But it should also be recognised that this was a worsted spinning mill and, despite local opposition, was as much an extension of the domestic industry as a factory system of production. What is more, it served not only the worsted industry, but also the cotton industry. This was in line with developments in the wider area of the clothing districts. In the Aire Valley, for instance, especially around Keighley, numbers of cotton spinning mills had been established in the late eighteenth century, some of which were converted to spinning worsted yarns at the beginning of the nineteenth century; High Mill at Addingham in Wharfedale had begun life in the same way, as a cotton spinning mill, but had been converted to worsted by the early years of the nineteenth century, while back in Bradford itself, John Rand had built a mill near to the site of the present Alhambra Theatre for spinning worsted and cotton in 1803. But the Holme deserves its iconic status, for it marks the beginning of the industrial era in Bradford and one that brought great changes in population and industrial growth that were replicated in the built urban environment. Probably the most radical years of change were the first forty years of the nineteenth century. During this time the numbers of factories increased annually, rising from one in 1800 to thirty-four by 1834 and sixty-seven by 1840.

This is a good point at which to explain one of the essential features of Bradford's textile success. Until the 1830s typical Bradford wool textile products were worsted yarns and fabrics, but by the mid to late 1830s a new kind of material began to be produced – Orleans. This was a mixed-fibre textile consisting of cotton warps and wool worsted wefts. Although reputed to have been developed in the 1820s, its production was limited because of difficulties in dyeing cloths formed of mixed fibres. By the late 1830s, Bradford manufacturers had been experimenting with the hair of the alpaca, eventually producing a cloth composed of cotton warps and alpaca wefts. What this gave was a stiffish cloth with a silky finish, a lustre cloth as it became known. Once the problem of dyeing mixed-fibre goods had been solved – largely by Ripley's dyeworks in Bowling – a textile revolution had occurred, and Bradford Orleans and lustre cloths were dress fabrics that remained in fashion throughout the middle years of the nineteenth century. In fact by 1850 further cloths were brought onto the market using silk or mohair rather than worsted or alpaca yarns. John James writing of this industry in 1857 recorded that the merchant houses of Bradford:

> 'took very large quantities of Alpaca stuffs, which began to be made in an endless variety of goods suited both for male and female dress, and including scarfs, handkerchiefs, and cravats, plain and figured goods, both with silk and cotton warp, for ladies dresses, dyed Alpaca checks of beautiful texture, and a variety of grogams, codringtons, silk-striped, checked, and figured Alpacas, and Alpaca linings.'[10]

Bradford had, he notes later in the same work, become unequalled for its production of such goods by any other town in the world.

This industrial expansion could not have been achieved without a rise in the numbers of people living and working in Bradford. While natural increases in the local population were responsible for some of the increase that took place during the first fifty years of the nineteenth century, internal migration and immigration was also responsible for the huge jumps that the population of Bradford made during this time. People came from other parts of Yorkshire, Lincolnshire, Lancashire or English counties farther afield. By the 1830s there were a small number of German immigrants. There was also migration from Scotland and Ireland, increasingly from the latter as the potato famine gripped Ireland from the mid to late 1840s. The population of the borough rose from 13,264 in 1801 to 43,527 by 1831, and it continued to rise by leaps and bounds until by 1851 it stood at 103,771 – a rise of nearly 700%. This made Bradford the fastest-growing industrial town in England and Wales in percentage terms in the first half of the nineteenth century, and it was well in excess of other towns in Yorkshire. During the same period Leeds had grown by around 220%, Halifax by around 180%, Yorkshire as a whole by 115%, while England and Wales increased by just over 100%. This sort of statistical picture puts Bradford's astonishing growth into perspective.

It is scarcely surprising that a more effective and organised form of local government was needed. Until the 1830s or '40s Bradford had creaked along under traditional and by then outmoded forms of administration. To begin with there was the legacy of the Middle Ages represented by the Ladies of the Manor and their rights in the town and its markets; there were the vestry officials – constables, church wardens, surveyors of the highways, overseers of the poor – who had limited powers; there were improvement commissioners appointed in 1803 with the specific duty of paving, lighting and watching the town, but only the area approximating to central Bradford. In other words, the fastest-growing town in the country had different forms of administration with weak powers that extended to limited areas of jurisdiction. The campaign to incorporate Bradford as a municipal borough and right this state of affairs began in 1843, but it was another four years before this was successful. Many Tories opposed the move towards incorporation, fearing rising rates and interference in civic life, but in the end liberal and reforming interests won the day and Bradford became incorporated as a municipal borough in August 1847. This permitted the division of the town into wards, and all male householders had the right to vote in an election for councillors.

By 1850 Bradford had changed in many respects. Its traditional formation as a small town with nearby villages had become that of an incorporated borough with a greatly expanded population; it had grown from a provincial cloth-making and market town to an industrial giant; its products – Orleans and lustre cloths – were in international demand. In addition to this there had developed a network of small foundries, engineering works and other small businesses, along with two major ironworks at Bowling and Low Moor whose products ranged from fire tongs and domestic grates to railway castings, boiler plates, heavy artillery and ordnance. Jonathan Glyde, a Congregationalist minister who had settled in Bradford in 1834, painted a brief but striking picture of the town and neighbourhood in a letter to his sister in 1835:

> The West Riding, in the very heart of which Bradford lies, is crowded with population and steam engines. Look which way you will, you see huge tall chimneys pouring forth volleys of smoke, which, when you are near, is not very pleasant, but when seen from a distance is interesting enough. There cannot be fewer than a hundred of these chimneys in Bradford and its vicinity; a cloud therefore is continually hanging over it; and this, together with the furnaces of the iron-works on the neighbouring hills, the flames from which though not visible by day become so by night...[11]

As hinted at in this passage, all this came with a cost and the price was paid in human and environmental currency. Bradford's lack of effective local government allowed developments that even by nineteenth-century standards were unacceptable. What is more, the infrastructure of the town built before 1800 was unable to sustain a rapidly expanding industrial population. A poor water supply, barely adequate drainage and a primitive sewerage system caused serious public health problems. Although most of the growing population was housed, types of housing and housing conditions varied from good to intolerable. There was much overcrowding and tenementing of older property, and a characteristic form of house for the working class was the back-to-back, often containing a separately let semi-basement or cellar dwelling. Large numbers of poor Irish immigrants inhabited this sort of housing in densely crowded areas of the town, the Longlands area at the top of Westgate near to St Patrick's Church being one of the worst. To add to these ills was the siting of factories in the middle of residential areas creating a smoky atmosphere which lingered in the bowl of hills that surround Bradford. In the midst of all this,

5 Bradford from the north, an engraving of the 1860s. This gives a good impression of the chaos of industry, housing and smoke.

providing entertainment, or oblivion for those who wanted it, were beer shops, dram shops, low music halls, singing saloons and prostitutes.

A further problem that arose was the social mix of this 'new' town. It was a town of strangers; a town teeming with people, many of whom had abandoned traditional ways of life to seek employment in mills or as domestic servants in the factory-town households of a callow middle class. This human impact shocked some of the professional families of Bradford, some of them, no doubt, experiencing large numbers of the working class at first hand and in an urban environment far removed from the cathedral or market towns in the agricultural districts of England. John Simpson, a young physician from Knaresborough who had set up practice in Bradford, seems to have experienced just this. Writing of Bradford in his journal in 1825 he found:

> There is no kind of Society here, every one being engaged in trade and thinking of nothing else. There are no pleasant rides, no pleasant walks, all being bustle, hurry & confusion. The lower order of people are little removed from the brute creation, being the rudest & most vulgar people under the sun. [12]

Jonathan Glyde, mentioned earlier, found Bradford a profound contrast to life in the south of England, the streets of the town filled with 'streams of young people of both sexes pouring along the streets at uncertain hours everyday … their manners rough, unpolished, uncouth, uncourteous'. At the same time, he maintained, there was a good deal of irreligion, large proportions of the population going to no service or church, 'but are either indifferent to the religion of Christ, or in too many cases grossly ignorant and immoral'. [13]

Yet if some sections of the population had abandoned religion, new identities and social allegiances were being formed through political action. While Bradford's growing trade in textiles was successful for some, there were, nevertheless, periods of depression and industrial unrest, especially in the 1840s. By that date also handloom weavers and hand combers were beginning to feel the effects of increasing mechanisation as wages fell. Factors such as this along with others such as dire living conditions made industrial towns like Bradford a fertile recruiting ground for political organisation, especially for Chartism. Radical political protest over the reform and extension of the franchise undoubtedly became entangled with more widespread feelings of discontent. Throughout the 1840s there were strikes and disturbances in the town, but none more severe than those of 1842 and particularly 1848 when serious rioting took place over a number of days, and the town was occupied by the Yorkshire Hussars, the 17th Lancers and the 73rd Foot who were brought in to restore order[14]. As one historian has commented, 'Bradford Chartists [in 1848] created a "no-go" area in the densely packed streets on the southern side of the town centre, from which they were able to defy magistrates, police and special constables for at least a fortnight'.[15]

However order was restored. It was disturbances like these and the state of the urban environment that prompted Titus Salt, the borough's second mayor, to institute an inquiry into the moral condition of the town in 1849. The general conclusion was that Bradford possessed shamefully overcrowded and filthy housing as far as the working class were concerned and that such conditions promoted immorality. Certain parts of the town were revealed as sinks of vice and iniquity – so bad, allegedly, that Salt refused to publish parts of the commission's findings. The solution was to provide moral leadership, respectable places of entertainment and foster a sense of civic pride and identity. This was a position that Glyde – who had been a member of the commission – alluded to in a sermon some time later at the funeral of a woolcomber:

> Strangers have poured into the town; some of us are strangers ourselves, knowing little of those around us, and unknown. We came here to do business and make money – have done it, and made it, and too little considered moral and spiritual relations ... we are awakening to these things, and, God helping us, we will improve. We will not only sustain our Infirmary, and a Park, and build our Music Hall, and shut up all cellars, and improve your cottages, and burn the smoke, and make the back as well as the front streets cleaner ... [16]

And so the passage continues. Sadly things did not go quite this far, but the spirit of Salt's commission did probably provoke unease in some quarters and it certainly did raise questions about morality and civic pride, so that from the 1850s the town began to change in some respects. What is perhaps not often realised is that the 'Victorian Bradford' that remains and is preserved today was a very different place from the Victorian Bradford of 1845. At that date the centre contained few public buildings other than the Court House and the Exchange, a reading room and public or assembly rooms built in 1827.

There were seventeenth- and eighteenth-century shops, small workshops and houses with other small nineteenth-century houses and shops squeezed into vacant plots behind older houses or on the main streets. There were many beer houses and dram shops, low music halls, tenemented buildings, lodging houses and foundries and factories. Amid this there was also a theatre and there were open markets and a cattle market that was held at regular intervals in the central streets. What is more, it was a town divided by a filthy stream, Bradford Beck. If little more than a trickle for much of the year, the Beck was nevertheless capable of swelling to a torrent and flooding after periods of heavy rainfall. By 1850 what middle-class families had lived in this crazy, contaminated centre had fled for the suburbs, returning only in daylight hours to places of work.

However, this urban centre did change. Investment by council and business leaders (often the same people) in public, civic and commercial buildings was one outcome. Amongst the first of this new generation of high-quality buildings were the Milligan & Forbes warehouse (now the *Telegraph & Argus* offices) and St George's Hall in Hall Ings in the centre of the town. Both were designed in lavish Italianate styles and, significantly perhaps, were located next to the town's most prestigious contemporary building, the Court House, built in the 1830s. The Milligan & Forbes building comprised offices and a warehouse, and the firm dealt in Bradford's textile goods; St George's Hall was the town's first public concert hall, a direct response to Salt's commission and alluded to in the passage by Glyde quoted above. By the late 1840s and '50s the railways had arrived in Bradford; the Midland and the Lancashire & Yorkshire Railways were to enhance the built environment further by building handsome terminuses in the centre of town.

The 1860s and '70s were a particularly busy period in the change of character of central Bradford with shops and chambers (offices) being built, covered markets being laid out, and the construction of what remain landmark civic and commercial buildings, among them the Wool Exchange and the Town Hall. At the same time much of the older town and with it some of the earlier factories were coming down, swept away by the rise of what the Bradford historian William Cudworth called 'Worstedopolis'. One of the more remarkable engineering feats is one that we are hardly aware of today: the culverting of Bradford Beck and other watercourses which today flow under the city streets. By the 1880s a great deal of the town had been remodelled. William Scruton, another Bradford historian of the nineteenth century, could write in 1889:

> So great a transformation has taken place, and the *old* has so completely given way to the *new* that anyone revisiting Bradford after an absence of a quarter of a century or so, would fail to recognise it ... The increasing activity of a wealthy and enterprising Corporation in the work of 'street improvements', has obliterated almost every trace of the 'old nooks and corners' ...[17]

The extent of the borough was also increasing by taking further neighbouring townships into its control – Bolton in 1873; Allerton, Heaton, Tyersal and

Thornbury in 1882; Thornton, Idle, Eccleshill, Tong and North Bierley in 1899. In 1897 Bradford had been created a city.

By the end of the nineteenth century Bradford had grown in size and in civic status. Yet despite the increasing body of local and national legislation concerned with the built environment, there remained many problems within the city. The council had inherited large areas of insanitary housing built before 1850 that continued to present health problems. Water supply was a further area of concern. Despite a council-owned water company and the construction of reservoirs near Grassington some twenty-five miles away, there were still problems. The nature of Bradford's industrial economy did not help, since it required immense amounts of water for the processing of textiles and for factory boilers. Although the cholera epidemics of the mid-nineteenth century had disappeared and the council boasted that the great majority of homes had a piped water supply on tap, the reality was not so rosy: in some districts domestic water was supplied via a standpipe in a yard; there were also droughts, serious ones in 1874 and 1884.

It was not until the first half of the twentieth century that these problems began to be tackled – council housing from 1909, and the extension of the water supply by the construction of reservoirs in the Nidd Valley. Other developments also led to changes in the city such as the establishment and extension of a telephone system and the increasing use of the motorcar. In fact Bradford had its own car manufacturer, Jowett, a firm that grew out of the engineering expertise of the city. Established in 1901, the company grew to produce vehicles with a national reputation for style and reliability before the company closed in 1954. Yet the character of the city, its economy and the problems associated with mass housing of the nineteenth century did not change radically until the second half of the twentieth century, and in particular from the 1960s onwards, despite council and private housing ventures in the interwar years. Indeed much of the twentieth century could be summed up as a reaction to the nineteenth century which took a long time before its effects on life in both great and small ways ceased – the last outdoor lavatories, a widespread feature of the district, were not eliminated until a drive in the 1970s, to give one small, yet significant, detail.

The real changes came on that wave of optimism that broke over the country in the post-war years. In common with several other towns and cities, the modernisation of central Bradford had been planned in the 1930s, but was halted by the Second World War. It was not until 1947 that the city engineer S.G. Wardley revealed plans for a new city centre to be constructed initially around Forster Square. It was a plan that called for the clearing of acres of land and the demolition of shops and textile warehouses, many of them of a high quality of design and construction. It was also a plan that was to lead to the enlargement of existing major highways until they became huge arterial roads cutting their way out of the city and obliterating residential areas at either side, replacing houses with tower blocks. Meanwhile the new centre would come to completion in a network of traffic flows, subways and high-rise modernism. A good deal of what was planned was generated by the car and keeping traffic flowing as much as in providing a new, progressive central business district and residential environs.

Bradford had been characterised by one lecturer in planning at the Leeds School of Architecture as 'a city planned by the Devil'; it was, he went on, a typical northern Industrial Revolution city that should be dismantled and re-planned. If this language was more colourful than most, even civic leaders of more staid and measured judgement were stirred into comment. Alderman R.C. Ruth, chairman of the council's Public Works Committee, wrote a long article in the *Yorkshire Post* praising the scheme and ending with the words:

> These are the plans of the future, and the progress and determination shown in the post-war years will surely ensure a large measure of achievement.

The new centre began to emerge in the decade between 1960 and 1970, yet not without dissent. If Nikolaus Pevsner – no lover of Victorian architecture per se – had in 1959 described central Bradford and the area around Forster Square as having 'no definite shape' and being 'surrounded by buildings of no distinction'[18], yet this scheme provoked him to write to the local papers in defence of the character of Bradford's central area which he saw as being overwhelmed by modernism and deprived of its unique character. Although by the 1960s the demolition gangs had moved in, the criticisms did not stop, and Wardley himself was forced to defend the plans – things were 'absolutely superb' he wrote to the local newspaper the *Telegraph & Argus*, and critics were asked to 'hold their fire'. Of course, by then it would have been too late, and was. In the absence of listings for the Victorian buildings of the city, and the deep disregard in which Victorian architecture was held at that date, not to mention the dazzling prospect that modernism seemed to offer, protest counted for little. Indeed, protesters might be portrayed as an obstacle in the way of 'progress', and progress was a word we heard a lot in the 1960s, although it was never clearly defined.

It is difficult to know what the majority of Bradfordians thought about these ten years of clearance and rebuilding at the heart of their city. Judging from comments in the press and vox pop interviews, while many people welcomed bright interiors and a greater range of shops, the design and planning continued to be viewed with suspicion verging on dismay. In 1967 Ian Nairn in 'The Glory that was Bradford', a programme made for BBC 1, savaged the planners, describing the new development as 'slab-sided monotony from end-to-end'. Perhaps the most poignant comment was made by a Mr W. Atkinson, aged sixty-two. When asked for a comment by a *Telegraph & Argus* reporter, he replied: 'It's no longer Bradford to me.'[19]

The rebuilding of Bradford was not the only significant event to take place in the 1950s and '60s. Bradford suffered a post-war labour shortage in the textile and other industries, and to fill the employment gap recruited workers from Europe, especially from Italy. Many Italian workers, mostly young women, came to the Bradford district, living either in hostels or lodging with local families. Immigration from Italy was added to by many eastern European families seeking shelter or asylum after the disasters of the Second World War. From the early 1960s there was also the beginnings of immigration from South Asia, largely from Pakistan. The first South Asian immigrants tended to be men coming to find employment in the textile industry. But by the later 1970s what might have been viewed earlier as a pattern of migrant working had changed to one of settlement here. Although links with Pakistan were maintained, families were raised in England, religious buildings constructed and businesses established. Unlike Italian and other European immigration which ended mostly in the 1950s, the South Asian population of Bradford continued to grow both by further immigration and natural increase.

Bradford by the 1970s had become a very different sort of place, but further change was on the way. The later 1970s and the 1980s witnessed the decline of the engineering and textile industries to the extent that only a fraction of either remains. Throughout the 1980s there were high levels of unemployment in the city and a bleak landscape of derelict works and mills that lingered through the 1990s. If things were not bad enough, racial tensions had reached breaking-point by the mid-1990s. Although the most serious rioting took place in the city in the summer of 2001, other disturbances had taken place in the 1990s with particularly serious rioting in Manningham in 1995. Even the riot of July 2001 was not the only one in that year. An earlier riot in April is sometimes forgotten, but illustrates the complexity of the situation. Initiated by white racists in the Ligate Green area of the city, it turned into a vicious clash involving not only the white initiators, but also Muslim against Hindu.

The subject of this book may be a history of Bradford's built environment, but the significance of its recent history of riots cannot be ignored: they are a landmark event in the city's history and they took place within this same built environment, parts of which they damaged or destroyed. Rather like the rioting of the 1840s and the reaction to it by the then council, it took the events of 2001 to make the city's leaders realise the dire state of its social relations and the shocking image that Bradford presents to the world. The watchword today is regeneration, and a good deal is pinned on yet another remodelling of the city. As I write, the 'absolutely superb' 1960s buildings in the centre are being torn down and are to be replaced by new shopping malls and offices. In addition to this, a plan for the refashioning of the whole of central Bradford has been commissioned, while many older buildings, warehouses and some mills are being restored and converted to other uses. It is too simple to draw a parallel with the 1840s and '50s where civic leaders sought to ameliorate the intolerable 'moral condition' of the town by building reforms and by a paternalistic control that propagated an ethic of respectability and civic pride. Today's approach is different and seems to be based more on an unqualified acceptance of cultural relativism and a belief that you can build your way out of social problems. The jury is still out on that one. But say what you like – fearsomely, perhaps foolishly, proud; racked by ethnic conflict and misunderstandings; desperately trying to re-invent itself – there is no other city in the country quite like Bradford.

2 BRADFORD'S EARLIEST BUILDINGS

There are good reasons why Bradford retains very few medieval buildings. Firstly, Bradford was not a densely populated town in the Middle Ages, but more of a market centre verging on a town, and consequently it possessed few religious and a relatively small number of secular buildings. Secondly, the area that became the borough was probably even more sparsely populated. In other words there were probably few buildings in total dating from between say 1200 and 1600. Thirdly, what had survived from this older stock of buildings almost certainly disappeared under wave after wave of development in the nineteenth century as the population rose and industrialisation carried on apace.

Nevertheless, there remain two major buildings of medieval origins in the city. The first of these is St Peter's, the parish church (the present cathedral). Although there is no mention of a church at Bradford in Domesday Book, this does not rule out the possibility, since the compilers of Domesday did not consistently list chapels and it is possible that Bradford's place of worship at this date may have been a chapel dependant on the church at Dewsbury. It can be seen from documents of the thirteenth and fourteenth centuries – such as an inquisition of the Earl of Lincoln's lands in Bradford in 1311 – that a church had either been built or possibly rebuilt; the Earl of Lincoln was the lord of the manor at this date. However, this was not the existing church which dates from a building campaign of the mid-fifteenth century to the sixteenth century. One of the problems in interpreting the present church is that many centuries have left their mark on it, but especially the nineteenth and twentieth when it underwent substantial remodelling and extension. Judging from the exterior, (2.1) the medieval parts of the church seem to date mostly from the Perpendicular period and from a rebuilding of the central body said to have been begun around 1430 and continuing until the 1460s.

The tower was probably added later and is said to date from between 1493 and 1508. The north side contains some of the original panelled tracery windows of the

2.1 St Peter's, the north side, mid-fifteenth century and later.

2.2 St Peter's, the tower, 1493-1508.

mid-fifteenth century, while other 'medieval' parts of the exterior are the result of nineteenth-century repair and rebuilding. The least altered part of the church is the tower (2.2), of sturdy construction and, like the rest of the medieval church, of local sandstone. It has, however, a rather weak castellated finish, although other detailing such as the double-louvred windows and the four-centred arched doorway is boldly and confidently executed. If the exterior of the surviving medieval parts of the church dates from the fifteenth century, earlier work can be found inside. Here the nave arcade seems to indicate the survival of an earlier structure of perhaps the early fourteenth century.

Set on a mound above the town and – in the Middle Ages – above Bradford Beck, the parish church must have been a commanding building prominent from several parts of the district. It lost this prominence in the nineteenth century when the new post office was built in front of it, and high-rise buildings throughout the city have diminished the importance of this view ever since.

The major secular medieval building in Bradford is Bolling Hall (2.4). The manorial history of Bradford after the Conquest is uncertain, but it seems likely that Bradford Manor consisted of Bradford, Great and Little Horton, and Manningham. At some time Great and Little Horton seems to have been created a separate manor, Manningham remaining part of Bradford Manor. The lords of these manors had residences there – at Bradford we know from surveys of the Earl of Lincoln's lands that it seemed abandoned in 1311 and in ruins by 1342. There was probably also a manor house in Horton Manor, but its location is unknown, and in any case these houses disappeared long ago.

Not so in Bowling. Bowling seems to have been a separate manor and was recorded separately in Domesday Book. Documentation of this early period is sparse and it is not until the later Middle Ages that a clearer picture emerges. We know from taxation records such as the Poll Tax return of 1379 that a family named Bolling was living there, and that they were not simply farmers, but seem to have been landowners of gentlemanly social standing – they are referred to as 'esquire'. It becomes clear also from documentation of this time that they were the lords of Bowling Manor. Their principal residence or manor house was Bolling Hall, a house and estate that passed to a family from Craven, the Tempests, by the marriage of Sir Richard Tempest to Rosamund Bolling in 1497. Much of the development of the house is bound up with these two families.[1] Bolling Hall is a complex architectural jigsaw that defies clear interpretation and contains a number of anomalies. Perhaps the greatest anomaly is that of the tower (2.3). This is a building of undoubted medieval origins: its purpose and detailing are the things that cause the problems. It has sometimes been called a pele tower, that is, a defensive tower or castelet such as those found in the Border Country. While it is ruggedly built of rubble, the openings in it could not seriously have been intended for defence. They are also of an unusual form – wide openings with mullions, but lacking any form of surround. Internally

2.3 Bolling Hall, the tower, late medieval.

the first floor contains a fine panelled chamber; it is heated, has an embrasured window with a seat and a jakes or lavatory which is contained in the turret to the left of the illustration. Comfort, rather than defence, seems to have been the purpose of this part of the building. Also, from internal remains, we can see that a timber-framed hall adjoined the tower.

Trying to recover the configuration of the medieval buildings on this site is by no means easy, since it seems likely that the medieval owners had remodelled the house, not to mention further remodelling by later generations. A general sequence of events may have been as follows. By *c.* 1300 the Bolling family were established in a timber house on this site. Perhaps around that date or as a reaction to Scottish raiding after Bannockburn in 1314 they added a stone-built defensive tower. As times became more settled, either Tristram Bolling or Sir Richard Tempest remodelled this tower as a 'solar tower', that is a tower built for private entertainment and comfort, but also as a mark of status. There were other buildings on the site, and one that was retained and has survived in part is the timber hall.

Bolling Hall did not pass out of Tempest hands until 1649 when Sir Richard Tempest sold the manor to Henry Saville of Thornhill in order to pay the fine imposed on the estate for Tempest's part in the Civil War. The present architectural form of the house is probably the result of still further rebuilding by the Tempests. It seems to belong to the late sixteenth or early seventeenth century both in terms of its style and the massing of its different elements.

An attempt seems to have been made to make the garden front – facing approximately the south – symmetrical by rebuilding in stone and by placing two-storey bay windows to either side of a central hall; a tower was added at the eastern end to balance the existing medieval tower to the west; the composition was thus framed between these two towers. It is the sort of design that we associate today with great Elizabethan architects such as Robert Smythson, and which became a common pattern for the design of grand houses amongst masons and architects until the beginning of the seventeenth century. The design does not come off quite so well at Bolling, however, partly because of the falling site and partly because of the inclusion of earlier elements, which lends a patchwork feel to the garden front (2.4).

2.4 Bolling Hall, the garden front, medieval and later.

By the beginning of the sixteenth century Bolling Hall was probably the largest house in the Bradford district. Other local houses of medieval origins rebuilt in the seventeenth century were the houses of the Sharp family at Little Horton Green – Horton Hall and Horton Old Hall. Both were large and impressive houses in their day, but both have now been demolished. Other houses of the seventeenth century have survived, some few of earlier origins. Just on the periphery of the city centre stands Paper Hall (2.5). This house was built, according to the date above the doorway, in 1643 and was the property of the Rooks family, a gentry family whose principal residence, Royds Hall, was to the south of Bradford. Paper Hall may have been built or acquired as a residence for younger members of the family. Its form and detailing is typical of the houses built by gentry or professional or merchant families of the district in the seventeenth century until about 1680. It is built of stone and has a central hall with cross-wings at either end. In addition the entrance is contained within a porch that blends into the wing. The hall and wing to the left (west) have windows that contain several lights created by runs of mullions, a constructional detail typical of the period. The wing to the right (east) is slightly different. This has windows in which the mullions form a cross, and what is more, they have triangular or semi-circular pediments above them. This sort of detailing indicates a date of probably after 1680, and it suggests that the wing may have been remodelled at around this date; but notice how one of the earlier windows has been retained in the gable.

2.5 Paper Hall, 1643 and later.

2.6 Little Horton Hall, Little Horton Green, mid-seventeenth century or later.

Paper Hall is the only seventeenth-century building to have survived within the old township of Bradford. There were undoubtedly others that survived until at least the nineteenth century, since old photographs and prints show them here and there among the buildings of the central shopping streets, especially along Ivegate. But development of the centre in the nineteenth and twentieth centuries has removed them all, and, because of the digging of deep foundations, there is unlikely to be any archaeological record, either. The best group of seventeenth-century buildings has survived in the street known as Little Horton Green at Little Horton. The Sharp family houses mentioned earlier stood in this part of Bradford. Perhaps the best of the seventeenth-century houses still standing there is Little Horton Hall (2.6) which was possibly rebuilt by the Lister family of Little Horton in the mid- to late seventeenth century. While the house retains the gabled elevation popular in the sixteenth and seventeenth centuries, it also displays some characteristics that represent a modification of, or a moving away from, that tradition – the high and carefully balanced arrangement of windows, for example. In its planning also there are further modifications – there are no cross-wings and the rooms are arranged in two rows behind one another, the so-called double pile plan. This was not a form of planning that one would expect to find in a gentleman's or a well-placed freeholder's house much before 1650.

Next door to Little Horton Hall is a good example of the sort of house built by small farmers and tradesmen throughout the district. Although 36 Little Horton Green (2.7) was converted to cottages in the nineteenth century, it dates substantially from the seventeenth century. A humble house, it has a distinctively elongated roof at the rear (2.8), sometimes called a 'cat slide roof' or in the local dialect an 'outshut'. Technically this is an aisle running the length of the rear on the ground floor, and probably providing space for a staircase and service rooms such as a dairy or 'milk house'. This left the two main rooms on the ground floor free: the hall or 'housebody' for everyday business and perhaps cooking; and the parlour, the private room of the master and mistress. Upstairs there were originally only two rooms, those above the hall and the parlour. This compact little aisled plan was once common around Bradford and can be found around Halifax and in the rural parts of the district.

While these two buildings probably represent builders at different ends of the social scale, what they both share is an earlier origin. Although both houses are substantially of the seventeenth century, both also contain indications that they stand on earlier sites and are the rebuildings of the houses that occupied them. In both

2.7 36 Little Horton Green, seventeenth century and later.

2.8 The rear of 36 Little Horton Green.

there are traces of older timber-framed construction, remnants that for structural reasons or economy in building were re-used as the new stone house rose around them. This is not to say that every sixteenth- or seventeenth-century house to have survived is based on an earlier one, but there are enough examples of re-used or intact timbers across the district to suggest a widespread tradition of timber houses, many dating back to the fifteenth century. Popular tales that these are ships' timbers are just that – myths.

Other houses were either completely new or their builders removed all traces of an older one. Such seems to have been the case with the house at Cousen Place, Great Horton. This consists of a long range of building originally containing three rooms in a line including a central hall. As often happened to older buildings, this offered a practical opportunity for conversion to a row of cottages in the nineteenth century, but much of the original detailing has survived to the rear (2.9), including a gabled wing. The wing may well have contained the best parlour to the front, and perhaps service accommodation to the rear. The doorway in the wing is a nineteenth-century insertion.

It is also clear that there was an aisle running behind the hall which was further extended in the early nineteenth century. The builder of the house is not known, but the original doorway, which has been walled-up, has the date 1657 and the initials W.E.S. This may stand for a member of the Swaine family, a family of substantial yeomen settled in the Horton district for several generations, and, if so, the house would be commensurate with their social standing.

2.9 Cousen Place, Great Horton, 1657.

2.10 Manor House, Rosebery Road, Manningham, medieval and later.

Perhaps the saddest sight among Bradford's early buildings is the so-called Manor House in Rosebery Road, Manningham (2.10). This was never a manor house in the sense of being the principal house within a manor, since for reasons mentioned above Manningham was part of the Manor of Bradford, but it has been the house of a person of means, nevertheless. Yet it is now only about half of the house it once was, because the widening of the road in the later nineteenth century resulted in the demolition of the right-hand (eastern) part of the house. The central part was given a new gable and some of the original detail seems to have been re-used in its reconstruction. It is now impossible to determine what its original form was, but it may well have had a central hall with a cross-wing at either end, or simply have had the present cross-wing and a longer hall range.

The present house is built of stone with a hall that has aisles both to the front and the rear: a house with a double-aisled hall like this is a rare survival in Bradford. What is more, this form of construction and the timbers of the roof suggest that here is the rebuilding of a medieval house of the fifteenth century or possibly earlier, having been rebuilt in stone in perhaps the late sixteenth or early seventeenth century. It stands a forlorn sight. Since its last occupant departed it has been boarded up; vandalism and the theft of stone from its roof have left it semi-derelict, a sad plight for a house of some character and antiquity.

3 AN EIGHTEENTH-CENTURY MARKET TOWN: BRADFORD 1680-1820

It is difficult today to think of Bradford as ever having been a market town, but that is how contemporaries saw it in the eighteenth century. Even as late as 1792, when we might regard Bradford at the beginning of industrialisation, the compiler of 'The Universal British Directory' could begin the entry for Bradford: 'It is an ancient and considerable market town'. When we think of a market town, a number of ideas come to mind about what such a town might contain and the business that might be carried on there. We should expect a marketplace, inns, a parish church and a mixture of houses, some dating back to previous centuries, others, usually those of merchants or the professional class of people, built to classical designs. Bradford, in fact, contained most of these features. Its marketplace was of medieval origins and regular markets were held there, and by the beginning of the nineteenth century a new classical building, the butter market, had been erected in Darley Street. By the end of the eighteenth century or beginning of the nineteenth, the town would have conformed pretty well to the above definition of a market town – there were shops, inns and a range of housing, much of it of three storeys; the parish church was a medieval church, as already discussed.

Yet this market town was different from some others in two respects. Firstly it is my contention that it began to develop such features only in the second half of the eighteenth century, and the expansion of the town with new buildings date from later in the century. Bradford is also a town built resolutely of stone and its builders never employed brick in the façades of their buildings, yet brick can be found in other Yorkshire towns even where sandstones and limestones are plentiful – at Tadcaster or Richmond, say. Secondly, as the compiler of 'The Universal British Directory' also commented, the 'staple trade of Bradforth consists chiefly of the manufacture of worsted stuffs'. This must have given Bradford something of the air of an industrial town also. Nineteenth-century historians such as William Cudworth recorded the memories of older generations who remembered this scene – a market town, yes, but one that also contained a small cloth hall, warehouses for textile goods and also further warehousing and trade carried on at inns in the central town. Yet so powerful was the development of the nineteenth century that it removed the physical remains of the eighteenth-century town and provided Bradford with a quite different identity.

Houses: A Changing Tradition

In the centre of Bradford Manor Hall or Bradford Hall once stood a classical baroque house. It was built for the Rawson family in 1707 and for most of the eighteenth century probably remained the finest house in Bradford. It was not until the second half of the century that Bradford's mercantile and manufacturing elite began to build on this sort of scale within and around the town – the Hustlers at Undercliffe and the Pollards at Tyrell Square, and perhaps best of all, the Bucks at Town Hill who had a house designed for them in the mid-1760s by the architect James Paine, just above the town on what is now Wakefield Road. All of these have long gone, swept away in Bradford's confident nineteenth-century expansion.

Very little of such house-building activity now survives, but one house that might stylistically be said to belong to this group is Boldshay Hall, built or rebuilt for the Hemmingway family in the first half of the eighteenth century.

Samuel Hemmingway was a lawyer who had acquired the Boldshay estate on the periphery of Bradford township by 1715. He died in 1733, having willed the estate to his son, Henry, who was also a lawyer. Boldshay Hall (3.1) has some pretensions for a small classical house. While its plan is simple and consisted of four to five rooms on the ground floor, the front contains the sort of detailing one would expect to find in the properties of great merchants or in small country houses of the period – large windows with moulded surrounds, and above all the doorcase displaying every trick

3.1 Boldshay Hall, 1715-40 and later.

in the architectural book – triangular pediment, over-scaled keystone and blocking to the architraves. Judging from nineteenth-century plans of the house, it seems to have been built with or to have acquired a large set of offices and stables to the rear and was set within small, but respectable, grounds. From surviving bills and accounts[1] it is clear that the building work was being carried out around 1740 by Henry Hemmingway. However, an undated letter of his father, Samuel, written to a friend in London, enquires about 'some glass for window sashes'. The explanation may be that it was Samuel Hemmingway that built the house, and his son added to or altered it.

At the opposite end of the century or perhaps the very beginning of the nineteenth, Edmund Peckover was to build Eastbrook House. Peckover was a member of a Norfolk Quaker family and had established a bank in Bradford in 1803, perhaps shrewdly realising the town's potential for commercial growth. Not so shrewd a choice was the site of the house on the eastern edge of the town – an open and pleasant landscape in 1800, but by 1850 on the edge of a smoky industrial metropolis which was to engulf it within a commercial landscape of warehouses. Strangely it survived, incorporated in a later building. The surviving garden front is shown at 3.2 with a central projection containing a mezzanine window which is flanked by two Venetian windows to the former ground floor rooms. Apart from the attic storey, the house is constructed of a fine ashlar sandstone.

Boldshay Hall and Eastbrook House are the only houses belonging to the eighteenth century that stand reasonably close to the city centre. To learn more about the architectural development of Bradford at this time, it is necessary to explore its

3.2 Eastbrook House, *c.* 1800.

hinterland, the townships that eventually were to constitute the borough, as well as some developments around the perimeter, for it is in these areas that some earlier houses can be found.

Typical of houses built by well-to-do tradesmen by the end of the seventeenth and beginning of the eighteenth century is the house known as John Hall's House in Great Horton (3.3). Hall was what we might regard as a master manufacturer, probably putting out work to local textile workers and marketing the finished products. He is also said to have been a carrier with a string of packhorses, according to William Cudworth. He was, in other words, a substantial man of trade, and his house represents this. Although built of local stone with largely traditional detailing, the main frontage displays a balanced arrangement and the house is built to a double pile plan. Also, the central entrance is given impact by a small classically derived pediment to the doorway and an oval window set directly above, hinting that by the time it was built – it is dated 1697 – the modification of earlier traditions was well advanced.

In the same emerging tradition as this house is Tree House Farm in Cutler Heights Lane (3.4). The detailing and its symmetrical arrangement suggest a date of around 1700. The windows retain the form of slim splayed mullions within a moulded surround typical of the seventeenth century, but the doorcase with its heavy plain lintel and jambs is rather different and changing to the sort of detailing that becomes common in vernacular houses of the eighteenth century.

The final changes can be seen at Far Oaks, Birch Lane (3.5), a house enmeshed in the later nineteenth-century development of Bowling. It dates from perhaps between

3.3 John Hall's House, Great Horton Road, Great Horton, 1697.

3.4 Tree House Farm, Cutler Heights Lane, *c.* 1700.

3.5 Far Oaks, Bowling, early eighteenth century and later.

1700 and 1740. Notice here that while the windows retain mullions, they are now square-faced and there are flat surrounds to the openings. The same doorcase as at Tree House has been used, centrally positioned with a heavy lintel, but there is an additional one, probably added as a result of sub-division in the nineteenth century when the house was occupied by two brothers, Thomas and William Benson.

This transition from moulded seventeenth-century detail to the plainer detail of the eighteenth century seems to have occurred between around 1700 and 1730, and there are some well-preserved examples in the wider Bradford district. One of the remarkable things about Bradford is the way in which traces of an earlier farming culture have survived within the built environment, almost like islands that became cut-off by the rising tide of nineteenth-century industrialisation. The most remarkable 'island' in the whole of Bradford is Little Horton Green. While not far from the city centre, this street contains houses of all periods from the late Middle Ages to the nineteenth century. As mentioned earlier, the Sharp family had been the principal landowners here, their last lineal descendant being Faith Sharp. She was responsible for further building or rebuilding on the estate and this included the house that has come to be known as Faith Sawrey's House – she had married Richard Gilpin Sawrey in 1722. Dating from 1755, the house (3.6) is a good example of a 'laithe house', that is a barn, byre and house under one roof, but with no internal communication between the domestic and agricultural sides. It is strongly detailed with the same

3.6 Faith Sawrey's House, Little Horton Green, 1755.

square-faced mullions and flat surrounds to the windows and doorway as above. There is also a date tablet with the inscription F.S. 1755.

More typical of the dwellings of the majority of people were older houses that had fallen into disrepair and had been tenemented. It is often not realised that in urban areas in particular the lower orders of society lived in tenemented buildings or under the same roof as their master and mistress either in attics or outbuildings or attached cottages. This is by no means the whole picture, however, and in rural areas that might make up the hinterland of a town like Bradford cottages and terraces of cottages were built, often by employers for workers or by small tradesmen themselves engaged in industries such as mining, quarrying or textiles. The row of cottages in Bowling Old Lane (3.7) was probably built between 1760 and 1800. Although converted to a public house by the early years of the nineteenth century, the row was possibly built for craftsmen and their families originally and displays fair detailing to the doors and windows and in its raised quoins or corner stones. At Horton Bank Top a small colony of cottages survives, possibly the homes of colliers (3.8). Once typical of the area was the long single-storey cottage to the front of this group; in the background are cottages of two storeys, one having a sundial with the legend 'Time doth fly, Man must die 1814'. The walling stone here is thinner and of poorer quality than we have seen previously, and many such cottages were originally rendered, or 'harled' to use a local term, in order to keep them weather-tight, as the single-storey cottage demonstrates. Nevertheless, with flag roofs often supported on oak timbers they are soundly built.

3.7 Bowling Old Lane, Bowling, 1760-1800.

3.8 Horton Bank Top, Great Horton, possibly early nineteenth century and 1814.

Houses of the Textile Industry

The trades and crafts that were associated with eighteenth-century Bradford were heavily textile related. As we have seen, Bradford had a piece or cloth hall from the 1770s drawing in textiles produced in its hinterland for marketing. While Bradford may never have had the grandeur or even range of housing that rested on textile wealth like its wealthier neighbours Halifax and Leeds, there were some families that rose to prominence as textile merchants or producers. If the best of the houses built have been demolished, some others survive.

At Hill End, Great Horton (3.9) stands a house built in 1714 probably by Thomas Hodgson, who seems to have been connected with both production and marketing. The house combines elements of both the classical and the traditional: the windows, which originally contained cross-mullions, have moulded surrounds, as does the doorway, and all are combined symmetrically. Yet the house retains an aisled plan and the walling is of coursed rubble. The date tablet contains the date 1714 and the initials T.H.M.

At Rosebery Road, Manningham is another house built by a master manufacturer or merchant (3.10). In 1786 Jonas Booth bought land and property in Manningham and built this house on the site. Booth described himself as a 'stuff manufacturer' which implies that he was putting out work to worsted hand weavers. To the rear stands a small warehouse. Again the house has a certain vernacular quality to it in its coursed rubble walling and the simple surrounds to the windows, but it is respectable enough. The gate piers are arguably the finest detail.

Typical of the independent worker or small manufacturer is Ashfield in Tong Street, Dudley Hill (3.11). The front of the house gives no indication of its use as

3.9 24.Hill End, Great Horton, 1714.

3.10 Rosebery Road, Manningham, 1786-1800.

a small textile workshop as well as a dwelling, but the rear (3.12) contains a now blocked taking-in door used for transferring raw materials and finished products to and from a first-floor shop, a common arrangement. As with many buildings of this age, some of the detailing has been altered by later generations of occupiers.

Not all clothiers or weavers were independent weavers producing cloth to take to market. Many were in the employ of a master manufacturer or merchant who put work out to them and collected it on an agreed date. Furthermore, as discussed in Chapter 1, not all textiles produced in the Bradford district were wool textiles. In Great and Little Horton the manufacture of cotton goods, chiefly calicoes, was carried on. A superb short row of cotton workers' housing has survived at Little Horton Green (3.13). These three-storeyed cottages are built of stone and boldly detailed with raised quoins and square-faced surrounds to doorways and windows which are divided into three lights. Notice how the taking-in doors give access to the first and second floors, suggesting that the greater part of this housing was given over to manufacturing with domestic accommodation perhaps largely on the ground floor. William Cudworth[2] relates that this row was built by Samuel Swaine, the Swaines being a Horton family with interests in both the worsted and cotton industries.

The topography of Bradford allowed some variation in the ways in which houses or cottages might be built. The apparently four-storey pair of cottages illustrated in figure 3.14 stand in Quebec Street and were probably built around 1800 as two separate units one on top of the other. Taking-in doors in their gable (now masked

3.11 Ashfield, Tong Street, Dudley Hill, second half of the eighteenth century and later.

3.12 *Above:* The rear of Ashfield showing a blocked taking-in door.

3.13 *Left:* Little Horton Green: cotton manufacture second half of the eighteenth century.

3.14 Textile workers' cottages in Quebec Street, *c.* 1800.

by later development) indicate their former use in textile production, although they had been converted to wool warehousing in the nineteenth century.

There must have been many more buildings and houses given over to textile production within the district, but not all are recognisable, since not all possessed taking-in doors and unlike some other parts of West Yorkshire, such as the Huddersfield area, Bradford textile workers' houses rarely seem to have been constructed with galleried windows to loomshops or other workshops. What is more, as continually stated in this chapter, large numbers of eighteenth-century houses and cottages were swept away in the rise of the nineteenth-century borough.

Public Buildings

Few public buildings of any sort were built in the Bradford district in the eighteenth century and even fewer have survived. The new market halls, built rather late in the period under discussion, did not survive above a generation or two before they were replaced and neither did the Piece Hall, although strictly speaking these were commercial buildings. There were several nonconformist chapels built, although only one survived the nineteenth century, to be destroyed in the twentieth century. One Anglican chapel remains and that is Bierley Chapel (3.15). It was originally a

3.15 Bierley Chapel, Bierley, 1766, John Carr.

3.16 Doorway to the former Public Rooms, Piccadilly, 1827-29, F.W. Goodwin.

private chapel built for Richard Richardson junior of Bierley Hall, and being built at the far end of his grounds fell just within the Bradford boundary. Erected in 1766 to the designs of John Carr, it is a small chapel with modest detail, the windows being contained within a series of blind arches. It makes its chief impact at the front, west, entrance with a pedimented gable and cupola above terminated by an obelisk on the dome. The chapel was enlarged to the north in 1828 when the portico was also added. It did not become a public chapel with its own district until 1864.

As discussed in the first chapter, Bradford did not acquire the institutions of a typical eighteenth-century town until rather late. Amongst the latest of these was the building known as the Public Rooms built at the bottom of what is now Piccadilly between 1827 and 1829. The Public Rooms supplied a public reading room, lecture theatre and a hall where assemblies could be held. The chief feature to have survived is the doorcase (3.16), a monumental Greek Revival design by F.W. Goodwin, consisting of a pair of Greek Doric columns supporting an entablature rather weakly decorated with wreaths.

But by the 1820s Bradford was rapidly changing and what the Public Rooms represent is an end of an older tradition of urban development. Soon after they were built they were frequented mostly by merchants and manufacturers and, according to William Scruton, became known as the Exchange for this reason. By 1867 the Public Rooms, or Exchange, had been abandoned and had become occupied by the Post Office. Their origins in the polite culture of the eighteenth century counted for little in a factory town like Bradford, where capital was king.

4 BUILDING A BOOM TOWN: 1800-1850

Where does the eighteenth century end and the nineteenth century begin? Not with a jolt in 1799/1800. Social institutions, the economy, as well the building styles of the eighteenth century continued well into the nineteenth century, but with diminishing strength in a town like Bradford where the dragon's teeth of *laissez-faire* industrialisation had been sown. Nevertheless, until the beginning of the nineteenth century and for some twenty or thirty years after, the Bradford district would have retained a rural appearance. A number of contemporaries testify to this as well as nineteenth-century historians such as William Cudworth or William Scruton. Cudworth could write that the Horton district in the 1830s still had houses with gardens and orchards alongside Manchester Road, and that the village of Great Horton was separated from Bradford itself by a large area of fields and 'a highway having many long and lonely stretches, which on a dark winter's night were a source of dread to the timid pedestrian'.[1] Some older inhabitants could recall that in the centre of Bradford 'rooks were cawing in the grove in Hall Ings'[2], while others, referring to Bradford Beck, related how they had caught trout 'in as bright a stream as any in Yorkshire'[3], and maps and plans of the district made in the first thirty years of the nineteenth century show gardens in the central area of Bradford. However, the historian Jack Reynolds also notes that a survey of Church lands taken in 1825 states that four acres of land close to the centre of Bradford could no longer be retained by the Church, because 'smoke from the different mills has rendered the grass or herbage unfit for cattle'.[4] The growth in the number of textile mills was discussed in the first chapter, but several other types of industrial undertakings should be added – foundries, for example. The mill, factory and ironworks were one of the chief causes of Bradford's growth as people flocked to the town to find employment in these expanding industries.

Industrial Buildings

The first textile mills that appeared in Bradford, and elsewhere, were carding and spinning mills. Put simply, carding is a process preparatory to spinning where wool or cotton is drawn through a series of rollers covered with prongs so that the fibres are drawn into slivers making them suitable for spinning. In the introduction, Holme Mill in Bradford (which was built by 1800) was described as having achieved an iconic status as the first mill to be built in the town. This is broadly correct, but subject to some qualification since others had tried to erect mills before 1800 – John Buckley in 1793, who had proposed building a spinning mill powered by steam close to the centre of town; while more significantly in 1792 the *Leeds Intelligencer* carried an advertisement for the sale of what appears to have been a carding mill at 'Brick Lane, near Bradford'.[5] Brick Lane was re-aligned in the late nineteenth century, but can be identified with the present City Road. The origins of Bradford's first textile mills are not so simple as some local historians have maintained, but one thing is clear: after Holme Mill was up and running in 1800 other mills followed. The Garnetts, Rands, Thompsons, Woods and others had all built textile mills in the town by 1820 or before and related industries were also being established – the Ripley family, who were to develop one of the greatest industrial dyeing complexes in the country, moved to Bradford from Halifax in 1805.

Several points need to be made about this early enterprise. While Bradford was to grow into the international marketplace of the worsted industry, a number of the first mills were both *cotton* and worsted spinning mills, such as Holme Mill or Rand's Mill. There is also a perception that development took place on a continuum from small, architecturally simple mills powered by water, to large, complex steam-powered ones. This is not wrong, but an oversimplification. Some of the first mills were large and powered by steam, but the expansion of mill sites in the nineteenth century and demolition in the following centuries has left few early mills intact, making an architectural assessment difficult. Holme Mill, for example, although demolished, is depicted in an engraving as four storeys in height and probably around twelve bays long (the distance between windows). It had a triangular pediment in the centre, giving a modest classical feel, and was steam-powered. When Waud's Britannia Mill was built in Bradford in 1836 contemporaries thought it to be of huge proportions, and although mostly demolished, map evidence of the site tends to confirm such astonishment. Again, although many of these early mills were built along Bradford Beck or its tributaries, this was not for water to power wheels, but to obtain water for processing or as a means of disposing of effluents. The old watercourse that supplied a number of Bradford's early mills can still be traced. This was originally a millrace or 'goit' cut from the Beck and running roughly parallel to it to drive water-powered corn and fulling mills of the previous century, but it was readily utilised by the expanding textile industry in the nineteenth century as a water supply. The area around here became known as Goitside and Water Lane.

There remain numbers of mills and warehouses, both large and small, along Thornton Road and Goitside, although much of what survives was rebuilt in the late nineteenth and early twentieth centuries. In amongst it are the remains of Thompson's Mill. By the beginning of the nineteenth century Benjamin Peile had established a dye works on Bradford Beck and had also financed his nephews, Benjamin and Mathew Thompson, in building a spinning mill around 1803. Over the years this was expanded by the addition and rebuilding of warehousing as well as combing sheds to form a much larger mill. A good deal of this earlier mill development has been demolished, together with the sheds. What the illustration (4.1) records is an historic site, looking across a cleared area in the shadow of the warehouse to fragments of the mill, and a further mill, Providence Mill, in the background; Providence Mill was another early spinning mill.

One or two other mills have survived rather better. Cross Lane Mill, Great Horton (4.2) was begun by Eli Suddards in 1821, but was taken over and completed as a spinning mill by James Cousen. This is a small mill that retains a vernacular quality derived in part from the coursed rubble of its walling. Bands neatly define the storeys and in the south gable there is a Venetian window. At the north end is a stair turret built like a little Italian campanile with its own hipped roof; narrow windows light the staircase. Over the years different owners have expanded the site, but the original spinning mill stands largely intact. Perhaps many of Bradford's early

4.1 The Thompson's Mill site, Tetley Street, looking towards Providence Mill.

4.2 Cross Lane Mill, Great Horton, 1821.

mills were of this scale, but what makes Cross Lane Mill different is the modest detailing which lifts it just above the ordinary.

Although the industry expanded and was to become more complex in Bradford with the introduction of Orleans, small mills continued to be built. Laneside Mill in Bartle Lane, Great Horton (4.3) was built in 1841. It comprises a long two-storey range and at one time a three-storey wing. There is little to relieve this almost unadorned frontage (the doorway is a twentieth-century insertion) except for the cart entrance, a large segmental arch springing from impost blocks and composed of a series of voussoirs with emphasised joints. The keystone is over-scaled slightly to allow for the inscription 'SSD 1841'. Samuel Dracup was a worsted entrepreneur of some invention, applying the technology of the jacquard loom to worsted production, while in the 1830s he had perfected the card-cutting machine essential to the operation of jacquards. Suddard also indicates a further facet of the textile industry of nineteenth-century Bradford: although engaged in the industry, this mill was probably a jacquard loom works, retaining this function for much of the century.

Some mills built for textile production were tenanted. Cannon Mill, Great Horton, was built by Samuel Cannan in 1826, and was let for 'room and power' to small businesses or sometimes larger ones needing further capacity. The original seems to have been a four-storey spinning mill, but a chimney collapse in 1839 resulted in a rebuilding in 1855, at which time it was owned by the textile merchant George Greenwood Tetley. The principal building was remodelled on its entrance face in an Italianate style by the Bradford architects Andrews and Delauney, although

4.3 Laneside Mill, Bartle Lane, Great Horton, 1841.

4.4 Cannon Mill, Great Horton, 1826, 1855 and later Andrews and Delauney.

it seems to incorporate some earlier work. The view shown (4.4) gives some impression of its extent from the rear where what are probably combing sheds of a single storey with saw-edge roofs have been added. What is missing is the chimney, which was demolished some years ago. Cannon Mill takes us just into another era, however, one where all the processes of worsted production had been successfully mechanised and when the Bradford Trade was entering its golden age. The industrial buildings that this produced are the subject of the next chapter.

The production of textiles was only one side of the industry. Another was the trade in raw materials and also in yarns and finished cloths. A flourishing commercial population grew up in Bradford composed of merchants from across Britain as well as from Germany. By the 1830s a distinctive area of warehousing was being erected near to the Public Rooms and in Piccadilly, the street running parallel to Darley Street. A typical example is shown at 4.5, a shot taken at the rear of a building in Dale Street. This shows how these four-storey warehouses were built in quadrangular form with an open courtyard in the centre – a further range having a cart entrance would

4.5 Warehouse, Piccadilly, 1833.

originally have closed-off the quadrangle. Offices to the front – and side in this case – contained the better detailing, having moulded surrounds to the windows. Above the eaves of this warehouse is the inscription 'Piccadilly 1833'.

What these new forms of warehouse, together with warehouses at mills, had tended to do was to eclipse older ways of trading and marketing. Woolstapling from private houses, meetings at inns along Kirkgate between merchant and manufacturer and the business of the Piece Hall was in steep decline.

Housing an Expanding Population: the Middle Class

The ways in which society began to change in the nineteenth century is a debate that continues to preoccupy historians and sociologists. While it is not a debate wholly appropriate to the subject of this book, it is one that must be taken account of, since social change, along with other factors, gave rise to different ways of living which are reflected in different forms of houses. It is probably true to say – if simplistic – that urban society of 1880 was very different from that of 1760. The old professional groups, together with one or two families of gentle birth that lived in eighteenth-century Bradford, had left or died out by the nineteenth century. In their place were new families who followed both traditional callings and also new ones, or lesser ones that had acquired a new status – the engineers or chemists, for instance.

4.6 Bolton Royd House, Manningham, *c.*1832 and later. James Richardby (?).

4.7 Melbourne Place, Little Horton, *c.* 1840.

Then there were British and foreign merchants, not forgetting entrepreneurs in the textile industry. These sorts of families formed an elite that was to fill positions of authority in the town, yet few lived within the central district and by the end of the century probably none, preferring villas in the suburbs of Manningham and Little Horton. One of the first of these suburban villas was Bolton Royd House (4.6) in Manningham built for J.G. Horsfall around 1832. Horsfall was a spinner and later a manufacturer of worsteds. This is a significant house, because it marks what was probably the beginning of the Manningham suburb.

When first built it stood within extensive grounds which in the 1850s and 1860s, after Horsfall's death, were sold for building land, a smaller area of garden being retained. It is built in a Greek Revival style, a bold Doric portico placed centrally, but somewhat overwhelmed by the pair of two-storey square bay windows that flank it. Further Greek-derived honeysuckle decoration can be found carved into the lintels of these windows. Later occupiers extended the house and added further decorative touches such as the iron crest above the portico.

The Greek Revival coincided with the last development of eighteenth-century classicism – neo-classicism, a more austere form with an almost archaeological attention to detail. The Greek Revival and neo-classicism persisted in England for about the first forty years of the nineteenth century. Bradford proved no exception in this respect, most of its first middle-class houses being designed in these classical styles.

This can be observed in a pair of semi-detached houses in Melbourne Place, Little Horton, the lower part of this district developing as a middle-class suburb in the mid-century after the sale of much land belonging to the Giles family after1839. These houses (4.7) were built in probably the early 1840s and are somewhat severe in their detailing. The beauty of the design is as much in the fine ashlar walling and the carefully proportioned tripartite windows which are relieved with some acanthus leaf decoration at the tops of their mullions. This same austerity can be found in some of the short terraces that were appearing in Manningham. On Manningham Lane is a terrace (4.8) similar to one designed by the Bradford architect Walker Rawsthorne and which appears drawn on a survey of land in this area dated 1836. Like the previous example, these houses are constructed of ashlar; they have heavy, yet plain doorcases supported on Doric piers, the windows above having lightly moulded surrounds to give further emphasis to the entrance.

This sort of detailing – austerely classical or Greek – could be used in mass-produced forms to lift the appearance of modest terraces intended for lower middle-class occupation. Giles Street (4.9), Little Horton, was built around 1854 probably as a speculation by the building contractors, Beanlands.

In most ways this is a standard Bradford row of the mid-century, built of local sandstones and using long, thin lintels above the openings. But Doric door surrounds with shallow triangular pediments and acroteria at each end have also been provided. This and the sweeping of the cill band lends a touch of humble elegance to an otherwise ordinary terrace.

With the possible exception of Giles Street, the houses illustrated so far have a certain urbane and classical character. Yet this was a taste on its way out by the 1830s and certainly by the 1840s, when Gothic Revival styles based on the architecture of the Middle Ages began to challenge the supremacy of classical styles. In Bradford there were probably no truly Gothic houses built until the 1840s, at any rate not in the high-minded ideological spirit of the Victorian Gothic Revival. However there were some Gothic designs. In 1825 Bradford's Wesleyan Methodists built Eastbrook

4.8 Terrace on Manningham Lane, Manningham, 1830-40s. Walker Rawsthorne (?).

4.9 Giles Street, Little Horton, *c*.1854.

4.10 Chapel Street, Bradford, 1825. Joseph Botham.

Chapel just to the east of the town, and along with it a pair of houses (4.10) for the ministers in what is now Chapel Street. All were designed by the Sheffield architect Joseph Botham in a Gothic style, but one that had its heart in the previous century. Although the doorways and windows have mildly pointed arches, the overall effect, if agreeable, is one of classical symmetry. Indeed, the piers to the doorcases, the cill bands, the mouldings to the windows and the panels below the ground-floor windows are all derived from classical sources. The Gothic appearance is created more by the intersecting tracery of the window glazing bars – notice the effect that this has in the right-hand house compared with the left-hand one where the glazing has been removed.

As far as Bradford is concerned, Gothic Revival designs of houses did not really penetrate the borough much before 1850. House styles for the middle class remained firmly fixed in the Greek Revival and neo-classicism.

Housing an Expanding Population: the Working Class

> The older portions of the town are built upon steep hillsides, and are narrow and irregular. In the lanes, alleys and courts lie filth and debris in heaps; the houses are ruinous, dirty and miserable ... In general, the portions of the valley bottom in which working men's cottages have crowded between the tall factories, are among the worst built, and dirtiest districts of the whole town.[6]

This is Engels's description of Bradford in 1845. Engels wrote of the nightmare conditions in which he found large numbers of the working class living in the mid-1840s in London, Manchester, Leeds, Bradford and other northern industrial towns. The conditions he wrote about were confirmed by national and local investigating committees, by journalists, by building inspectors and by medical officers. The surroundings in which many working-class families lived were indeed atrocious: no pure water supply, no adequate sanitary provision, overcrowding and pollution. Such a situation had arisen because of a number of factors such as a rapidly growing population, increasing industrialisation and, particularly, the lack of an effective structure of municipal control. At the beginning of the nineteenth century Bradford was governed by parish officials with limited powers, the remnants of manorial authority, and Improvement Commissioners appointed following the 1803 Bradford Improvement Act for lighting and watching the town. None of these bodies had overall control, nor were there any controls over building development generally. The result was the sort of chaos that Engels describes.

There were different ways in which this influx of working families and others were accommodated: by tenementing old buildings, by in-filling yards and gardens with cottages, by expansion along existing roads or by the building of 'colonies' of

4.11 Cottages in Great Horton Road, Great Horton, *c.* 1800-1825.

cottages by mill and factory owners, often near to mills and often on the edges of towns. From the beginning of the century rows of cottages began to be built on the major routes out of Bradford towards the borough townships, and vice versa. A typical grouping of such cottages is illustrated (4.11), cottages built piecemeal probably between 1800 and 1825.

Near the junction of Thornton Road and City Road (formerly Brick Lane) industrial developments had been taking place since at least the 1790s, and by the beginning of the nineteenth century rows of cottages had begun to appear. The row of cottages at Fearnside Street (4.12) is a well-preserved example dating from perhaps the first quarter of the nineteenth century. It may well have been built in connection with one of the mills in this area.

Mortimer Row on the other hand (4.13) dates from 1831, and may well have been built as a speculation by one of the Mortimer family, woolstaplers of Bradford Moor[7]. What all of these cottages show is a strong continuity of regional traditions of architecture. They are all built of local sandstones, have flag roofs and have mullioned windows with flat-faced surrounds; these also extend to doorways. Only at Mortimer Row is there a difference: although the windows retain mullions, the jambs are not lined with stone to form a complete surround, a development arising, perhaps, from the wish to make economies in building materials.

Most of these cottages have survived because they were well built and constructed from the excellent local building stones. What have not lasted are the gerry-built cottages. Where all of these cottages tend to fail is in their originally poor sanitary arrangements and restricted accommodation. Smaller, and even in their day less acceptable, were the sorts of single-storey developments often crammed behind

4.12 Fearnside Street, Thornton Road, *c.* 1800-1825.

4.13 Mortimer Row, Laisterdyke, 1831.

4.14 Farside Green, Little Horton, 1800-1830.

houses fronting the main roads. At Farside Green, Little Horton (4.14) is a rare survival. Built of traditional materials and originally with traditional detailing this is an area of single-storey cottages whose first occupiers appear to have been colliers, although by the 1850s and '60s they had a higher residence of people employed in the textile industry. Originally the roads would not have been surfaced and there was little or no sanitation.

Housing such as this was often brought into being by employers and building speculators. However, we should also be mindful that some of this sort of housing was of good quality and even some poor-quality housing might be brought into being by organisations such as building clubs or societies. The building club with working-class members seems to have come into being in the late eighteenth century, and there is evidence in Bradford that this happened during the early years of the nineteenth century. Such clubs or societies enabled people lower down the social ladder to obtain loans by way of mortgages in order to build houses. Street names that contain the word 'club' or 'union' are good indications of such origins, for example Club Street at Lidget Green (4.15). The detailing of this terrace suggests a date of perhaps the 1820s. It remains vernacular in appearance and has gardens to the front, originally with privies at the street end to allow the removal of refuse and sewage from the middens. They were built without backyards and there were no rear doors

4.15 Club Street, Lidget Green, around the 1820s.

– to use the local parlance they are 'through-by-light'. The original occupiers seem to have been minor tradesmen and textile workers.

However, not all was new build. Older houses might be subdivided and turned into tenements or back-to-backs. Knight's Fold in Great Horton is a house dating from around 1650-1700 that has been divided into four cottages and a new front added to the rear of the original house (4.16). The Knights owned a nearby cotton spinning mill which went out of business in 1826. It is likely that the house and land had belonged to them and that the division into four cottages built back-to-back dates from between 1800 and 1825.

At Knight's Fold four cottages have been created out of one house to produce a block of back-to-backs, but the back-to-back in Bradford was often built into

4.16 Knight's Fold, Great Horton Road, seventeenth and nineteenth centuries.

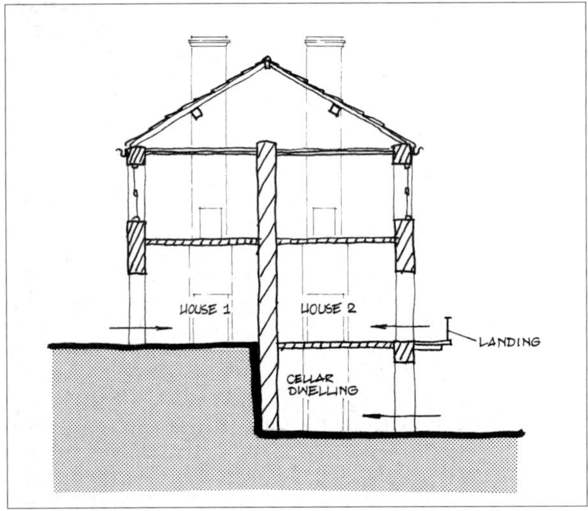

4.17 Cross-section of back-to-back cottages with cellar dwelling under.

terraces. Add to this the steep-sided valleys in which Bradford is situated and there is the potential for tucking further cottages under the row of houses built where the land falls away – a cellar or under-dwelling. The illustration (4.17) shows a common practice in Bradford of running a landing above the cellar dwellings to give access to the cottages above. Back-to-backs were the most despised form of housing in the nineteenth century. This arose from a mistaken view of how diseases spread. Air in the vicinity of rotting matter or confined air became degraded and was harmful. If this miasma, as it was known, were inhaled, it would cause illness, even death. Back-to-backs, having no rear doors, could not be 'through-ventilated', to use the medical jargon of the day. Hence miasma built up and diseases spread. The problem with back-to-backs was not miasma, but overcrowding, or being built around confined courtyards with privy blocks in the centre so that human sewage might contaminate the court or even the water supply – where one existed at all. There were numerous back courts and small crowded streets in Bradford by 1850, often with unmetalled roads that were dusty in summer and muddy in winter, with little or nothing in the way of pure water, and with primitive sewerage based on privies that discharged into an adjacent ashpit where ashes and household rubbish was thrown, then emptied by operatives known as night soil men, shovelling out the contents and carting them away.

None of these courts now survive, and very few back-to-backs of before 1850. Of those that do, they are little different in their appearance from the small terraces already illustrated except that they were built backing onto another row and usually had a narrow passageway connecting front and back. It is now hard to believe that such housing conditions existed, especially close to or even within what we now

4.18 The Duchess of Kent, Sackville Street, 1849.

consider the central business district. By 1850 the middle class were building houses in Little Horton and Manningham, but central Bradford, despite the beginnings of a more refined commercial district along Piccadilly, became an unwholesome amalgam of earlier buildings, shops, mills, foundries, bad housing, dram shops and beer houses. All was to change and very little remains today, although Sackville Street in the centre of town retains an inkling of this former appearance, including a few tiny cottages and what was the Duchess of Kent (4.18), built as a beer house in 1849 after the magistrates refused a full licence[8]. It is built of the same thinly coursed sandstone rubble as much of Bradford's cheaper building at this time, although the doorway with its elaborate surround and the large ground-floor windows tell us that this was more than a house. It typifies the main type of entertainment that was open to the working class. Along with this, sometimes a part of the larger establishments, were the singing saloons and cheap music halls. Again, all architectural remains have vanished, but anyone wishing to learn the character of these places should read James Burnley's *Phases of Bradford Life*, the chapter entitled 'The Dram Shops', which paints a vivid picture.

Churches

The massive and sudden rise in population made its effects felt not only on housing but also on religious provision. Of course this was not a problem limited to Bradford, but a national issue and led to the Church of England creating new dioceses and building more churches to accommodate the ever-increasing populations of industrial towns. The Church Commission had been established in 1818 with the object of building more churches. While this movement affected some outlying areas – in 1825 Shipley, a part of the parish of Bradford, was created a parish in its own right together with a new church – new Anglican churches in Bradford itself were built largely through private subscription. Such churches as Christ Church, Darley Street, 1815; St James, Manchester Road, 1838; St John, Manchester Road, 1839; and St Jude, Manningham, 1843, chart the progress of Anglican church-building in Bradford. All these have now been demolished. Very few of the pre-1850 Anglican churches of Bradford have survived. There are only St Paul, Manningham, 1848, built to the designs of Malinson and Healey and making provision for Anglican worshippers in the growing suburb of Manningham, and St John, Wakefield Road, Bowling (4.19). This latter church was built in 1842 and designed by R.H. & S. Sharpe of York. Unusually it was built as a 'company church' by the Bowling Iron Company to serve the district in which many of their workforce lived. It is a simple and dignified design relying heavily on the use of lancet windows and the impact made by its tall, slim spire. Internally it is also unusual for the nave arcade is constructed of cast iron, the architects being assisted by the Bowling Company.

4.19 *Above left:* St John, Wakefield Road, Bowling, 1842, R.H. & W. Sharpe.

4.20 *Above right:* Salem Chapel, Manor Row, Bradford, 1835.

It was not only the Anglican Church that was increasing provision. The same could be said of other faiths or denominations. The Roman Catholics had built their first church in Bradford, St Mary, in 1825 at Stott Hill, but this church was closed and moved to a much larger site later in the century. Of the nonconformist chapels, while many have survived, they are mostly post-1850. One exception is the Salem Chapel (4.20) in Manor Row. Built in 1835, it shows a strong Greek Revival influence in the Manor Row front, the entrance being pedimented and supported on Greek Ionic columns. The whole of this frontage is finished with a sturdy triangular pediment at the gable, stopped by acroteria at each end.

The Bradford of the first half of the nineteenth century is difficult to imagine either socially or spatially. While industry and commerce began to flourish and an affluent middle class began to emerge, there was also a large and increasing class of industrial workers. While for some life was organised around the daily routine of the factory and Sabbath-keeping, there were those whose lives were framed by drudgery, poverty, drunkenness and violence amongst a terrain of squalid houses and dark courts. It was amongst these narrow streets that the riots of 1842 and 1848 took place, for there were also sections of this working class that were beginning to organise politically. It was this social and physical disorder that civic leaders were determined to cleanse Bradford of, and over the next fifty years a different town began to be constructed.

5 BUILDING A VICTORIAN CITY: 1850-1914

The Moral Environment

In 1851 St George's Hall (5.1), Bradford's first public concert hall, began to rise on a site in Hall Ings. It was in many ways a significant building. Architecturally it was a fine building, but it was also one that represented a break with older traditions. Unlike its neighbour the West Riding Court House (demolished) or the Public Rooms, it was designed in an Italianate style rather than the Greek-based neo-classicism of the others, which belonged to a different tradition. It was designed by Lockwood & Mawson, an architectural practice new to the town, yet one that in the next twenty years was to become regarded by many as the finest. Politically it represented the determination to right the social evils of the town, especially the way in which matters had come to a head in 1848: this was Jonathan Glyde's 'music hall' in the sermon quoted in the first chapter, part of the solution, as Glyde saw it, to 'the social problems which now embarrass and prevent our happy progress'[1]. It was an attempt, in other words, to provide a sober and respectable place of entertainment, and entertainment of a morally uplifting kind, unlike the dram shops and beer houses. Whether that aim was effected is another question. Certainly some of the more educated sections of the working class of Bradford attended events at St George's Hall, but many more continued to drink themselves into oblivion. There are indeed two well-observed and contrasting sketches in James Burnley's *Phases of Bradford Life* – 'At a Subscription Concert' and 'The Dram Shops' – which tend to confirm this, if anecdotally.

Yet St George's Hall was symbolic of that change of mood in the city. If promoted and built by the town's business leaders, it was intended as a place of entertainment for the whole population of Bradford, and Lockwood & Mawson produced a design on a scale that matched these ideals. The architects have used as their model the sorts of urban palaces built for the Italian aristocracy in Northern Italian towns

5.1 St George's Hall, Hall Ings, Bradford, 1851-3. Lockwood & Mawson.

and cities of the sixteenth century. Here the design is adapted to a public hall and given an ornamental treatment in the finish of both its interior and exterior that the somewhat more austere originals did not have.

The important point about this building is its embodiment of these architectural and political ideals. It was the first in a range of public and commercial buildings that began to appear in the centre of Bradford as older, dilapidated housing and some factories began to be razed to the ground, all of which contributed to a sense of civic pride amid rising commercial prosperity in the second half of the century.

Public and Commercial Buildings

St George's Hall apart, Bradford's other major public building is the Town Hall. Bradford gained the status of a municipal borough with the powers to elect a council and levy rates in 1847. Until the 1860s, however, its business was conducted at a rather small and unpretentious building in Swain Street, an area of the city now completely lost in twentieth-century redevelopment, but in the vicinity of the Broadway. It was not until the late 1860s that a proposal to build a Town Hall which reflected the commercial and civic importance of Bradford was adopted. This perhaps highlights Bradford's sudden rise to prominence as an industrial and

5.2 Bradford Town Hall, 1873 and later. Lockwood & Mawson; R.N.Shaw.

commercial town of stature – Manchester had had a fine classical Town Hall since the early nineteenth century, while the Town Hall at Leeds was completed in the 1850s. Bradford Town Hall was opened in 1873, local architects Lockwood & Mawson having won the competition for its design.

This was not without controversy, for they were accused in the journal *The Architect* of plagiarising William Burges's design for the Law Courts in London which had been published in 1867. A good deal of ire spilled over the pages of the architectural press concerning these allegations, but in the end came to nothing.

What Lockwood & Mawson produced could hold its own with any of the great Gothic Revival Town Halls of northern England. It was eclectic in the way that it combined Italian and French Gothic. The main range of building draws on French models – the architects maintained that Amiens Cathedral was their inspiration – while the striking 200-foot tower above the entrance is modelled on that of the Palazzo Vecchio in Florence. Unusually amongst nineteenth-century Town Halls is the series of niches running the length of the building and containing statues of the kings and queens of England. The statute of Oliver Cromwell is said to have been included as an offering to strong nonconformist opinion. What has rarely been commented on is the pair of statues flanking the entrance: Elizabeth I and Victoria (5.3). The point being made here is perhaps the parallel between the imagined days of 'good Queen Bess' and Victoria: England prospered under both Queens and became great.

By the late nineteenth century the Town Hall was becoming too small for the amount of business conducted there and an adjacent site was bought. Here an

5.3 The entrance to the Town Hall.

extension was planned and built to the designs of R.N. Shaw between 1905-09. Shaw's work, again, makes use of the Gothic and although charged with designing a large extension at a later period his work, nevertheless, echoes that of the earlier (5.2).

If the Town Hall was the centre of municipal life, it had its commercial counterpart in the Wool Exchange (5.4), built a few years earlier. From a town little-known outside the clothing districts of Yorkshire in 1800, Bradford had become the international marketplace of the worsted industry and a centre of mercantile business for the West Riding by the 1860s. The Wool Exchange provided a floor on which the raw material was brokered and a trade carried on and prices fixed for almost any kind of wool or hair used in the clothing industry. The building and its origins were not without incident and ceremony. No less a figure than Ruskin was invited to Bradford in 1864 to lecture on what the commercial elite of the town had hoped would be a suitable design for the Exchange. However, Ruskin, typically perhaps, refused to be drawn, accusing his Bradford audience of caring more about commerce than art, and simply wishing to do the right thing architecturally. He did, nevertheless, suggest that the Venetian Gothic of Alfred Waterhouse's Assize Courts at Manchester was an example worth emulating. The competition for the design was also regarded as a dubious affair and one in which Lockwood & Mawson's plans were regarded as a foregone conclusion for winner. Indeed, they were to beat off competition from national figures such as William Burges and R.N. Shaw. Lord Palmerston laid the foundation stone in 1864 and in another three years the Wool Exchange was completed.

5.4 The Wool Exchange, 1867, Lockwood & Mawson.

The building occupies an awkward central site – wedge-shaped and on falling ground – to which Lockwood & Mawson had to adapt their design. If, indeed, they had taken heed of Ruskin's advice, the Wool Exchange does not owe much to it, having less in common with Venetian Gothic and more in common with the architecture of medieval Flemish cloth halls in its arcade of pointed arches to Market Street and a decidedly Flemish-looking entrance tower. All this has been achieved with a lightness of touch – the use of red and buff sandstones and the pierced parapet running around the roof help to create this impression. The building is also busy with symbolism, both local and national: along the Market Street front are reliefs set in rounds of eminent men. Titus Salt, founder of the trade in mixed-fibre Orleans, finds himself in the company of Cobden, Gladstone and Palmerston, figures associated with free trade and the commercial modernisation of the state; while at the entrance, older traditions are evoked in the figure of Bishop Blaize, patron saint of woolcombers and a reminder of a noteworthy saint's day in Bradford's past. The Wool Exchange also marks a decided change in Lockwood & Mawson's style from a largely classical Italian style to an eclectic Gothic. Their design of the Wool Exchange allowed for not only the Exchange floor, but also chambers (offices) above, and the firm were to move their architectural practice to chambers there – a significant move, perhaps.

Market Street in Bradford had begun to develop as one of the principal commercial thoroughfares of the town. Eventually the vista along this street was stopped by the tower of the Town Hall while the Wool Exchange was located about halfway along from the railway station, and in between were other well-designed buildings, several of which fell victim to demolition and redevelopment in the 1960s. Commerce, however, flourished in other parts of the town and was given similarly strong architectural expression, nowhere more so than in the warehouses that crowded round and between the town's two rail heads. This area stretched from Vicar Lane to the centre of town, and the area that we know today as 'Little Germany' is only a part of it, but one that has survived. Little Germany was so named because of numbers of German merchant houses setting up business there. The Behrens warehouse (5.5) is typical, being designed in a palazzo style derived from the urban palaces of Renaissance Italy. The first couple of storeys are strongly detailed while the upper three are much plainer before the whole is finished with a bold eaves-cornice.

Not all the merchant houses built here were owned by Germans or traded with Germany. The Law Russell warehouse or the Thornton, Homan warehouse (5.6) are two, the latter, for example, trading with America and China. They are both designed

5.5 S.L. Behrens & Company Warehouse, Peckover Street, 1873, Milnes & France.

5.6 Foreground: Law, Russell warehouse, Vicar Lane, 1873. Background: Thornton, Homan & Company warehouse, 1871, both by Lockwood & Mawson.

in a palazzo style as are the majority of warehouses in this area. But here the richness of detail and the quality of the craftsmanship reaches its height, the Thornton, Homan warehouse in particular has a carefully graded sequence of windows from the heavily rusticated at ground level to much plainer segmental windows on the fifth floor, giving a solid yet dignified quality to the building. What impresses most about all of these is their great scale, and yet they are crammed into a grid of narrow streets, their cornices and long registers of windows creating remarkable perspectives.

The 1870s marked the building of the last of the great textile warehouses in this part of the town, but further warehousing – mostly wool warehousing – was built as parts of Bradford in the Silsbridge Lane and Brick Lane areas were cleared of poor housing and these roads realigned to become known respectively as Grattan Road and City Road. While architectural historians have rightly identified the textile warehouses of Little Germany as worthy of comment, less attention has been given to later warehousing, some of it of outstanding quality. Woolston Warehouses (5.7) built for James Hill in 1903 to the designs of Rhodes Calvert proves the point. They are a typical late palazzo style with an elaborate doorcase employing grey granite Tuscan columns to frame the entrance and support a pediment in which a richly fleeced sheep stands. In the windows above, green granites are used. This polychrome effect together with rustication of the sandstone walling gives a hard, rugged feel to the building.

5.7 Doorcase at Woolston Warehouses, Grattan Road, Bradford, by Rhodes Calvert, 1903.

The prosperity of mid-nineteenth-century Bradford may have been brought about by the textile industry, but it also generated success in the commercial banking sector which also produced some fine buildings. One of the outstanding Gothic Revival buildings of central Bradford is the former premises of the Bradford Commercial Bank (5.8), which dates from 1868. It stands in Hustlergate near to the Wool Exchange and was designed by the Bradford firm of Andrews & Pepper in a somewhat French-influenced Gothic style, a tall tower with a mitre roof giving emphasis to its corner position.

The industrial boom of the nineteenth century also produced a revolution in transport, and Bradford was no exception here. The railways had made inroads into the town by the mid-century, the Midland, Great Northern and Lancashire & Yorkshire Railways all having stations here, stations of which hardly a scrap remains today other than some walls and embankments. But what the railways also introduced, which is sometimes forgotten, is the 'luxury' hotel in an age when travel was growing and the need for accommodation pressing. In Bradford as elsewhere, new hotels were often built by private enterprise. Firstly there was the rebuilding of existing inns to better standards – the Talbot in Kirkgate is a good example redesigned by Andrews & Pepper in 1878 in a palazzo style. But there were others, built from new, such as the Royal Hotel, Darley Street (5.9). This was built in 1887 to the designs of James Ledingham, a Bradford architect of Scottish extraction who had worked in the Andrews & Pepper

5.8 The Bradford Commercial Bank, Hustlergate, Bradford, 1868, Andrews & Pepper.

5.9 The Royal Hotel, Darley Street, Bradford, 1887, James Ledingham.

5.10 The Midland Hotel, Cheapside, Bradford, 1885, Charles Trubshaw.

office. It typifies Ledingham's sometimes rumbustious style which is based largely on northern Renaissance forms of architecture with steep pediments, Dutch Gables and arched panels framing the upper storeys.

But it was perhaps railway hotels like the Midland (5.10) that introduced luxury accommodation to the travelling public. The census entry for 1901 for the Midland Hotel gives some idea of the complex social mix of Bradford by the end of the nineteenth century, a place where business was transacted on an international scale: the manager of the hotel was German; waiters came from England, Scotland, Germany and Italy; there were two French chefs; guests were from England, France, Germany and America.

No survey of the commercial buildings of the town would be complete without the inclusion of shops. The development of a central business district in Bradford had led to the construction of new shops as well as buildings such as those mentioned above. Two stores were outstanding, partly because they were the first of what might be called department stores, but specialising in fabrics and home furnishings. Brown & Muff's was a business that remained in the city in the same building until the late twentieth century. The company's new store was opened in 1870 and designed by the architect George Knowles with a frontage to Market Street. The other was not far away, occupying a corner site at the bottom of Ivegate. It was designed by Thomas

5.11 *Left:* Thorpe Buildings, Ivegate, Bradford, 1871, Thomas Campbell Hope.

5.12 *Below:* The Arcade, New John Street, An arcade no longer, but a clothes store – this upper turreted window retains part of the stone lettering. Notice how the lintel is also supported on slim cast-iron columns.

Campbell Hope for George Thorpe in 1871, and Hope made a great deal out of the corner entrance (5.11) with a quadrant entrance and balconied window to the first floor whilst the second and third floors are simply canted across the corner. The whole design is in an Italianate style and a feature worth noting is the clustered arrangement of dormer windows and panelled chimneystacks above the eaves creating a busy roofline. The display windows have also survived and been restored to something like their original size. Reinforced timber beams and steel joists had come into use during the nineteenth century, making it possible to span large openings like these to provide space for display. What it acknowledges is the growing appreciation of shopping as a leisure activity. This was especially true of some of the larger stores in the centre of town and in some of the arcades that began to appear in the second half of the century, now either demolished or converted to other uses. These were the grandest of the commercial buildings to be found in the centre of Bradford, but shops and shopping were important throughout the borough. While many shops were the conversion of earlier buildings, perhaps the largest group of purpose-built shops in nineteenth-century Bradford were those built by co-operative associations. Co-operation had been a feature of working-class life in Bradford since the 1840s, although it is perhaps fair to say that it was not firmly established until the 1860s when a number of societies opened permanent shops; by the 1870s and '80s many branches were being opened. There was an increasing pressure from members to open more branches. The rather quirky-looking building in Great Horton Road (5.13) illustrates such a shop opened by the Great Horton Industrial Society. This was the Cannon Mill branch and café opened in the second part of the century to provide greater convenience to people living in the lower part of Horton, especially women who, one member wrote, 'were made into beasts of burden'[2] by the distances they had formerly had to carry shopping. It provided not only a store in the Italianate building in the centre, but also a café in the single-storey building to the right which took in the older cottages behind. It is remarkable that this humble structure survives at all.

Co-operative societies in Bradford continued to open branches throughout the nineteenth century and a mature example of a co-operative store is illustrated in Branch 37 of the Bradford Provident and Industrial Society on Manningham Lane (5.14). Built in 1898 it has a well-preserved shop front of that time, even, perhaps, to the blackening of the stonework, an appearance that all of Bradford's nineteenth-century

5.13 Cannon Mill Co-operative store and café, Great Horton Road, Great Horton.

5.14 Branch 37, Bradford Provident and Industrial Society, Manningham Lane, Manningham, 1898.

buildings acquired in its polluted atmosphere: most have now been cleaned. It is typical of that northern renaissance style popular from the 1880s with its tall curvilinear gable surmounted by a triangular pediment. The ground floor front remains intact, also.

Entertainment

The main form of entertainment for many in Bradford remained drinking. Also Bradford's civic leaders never quite rid the town of its disreputable drinking places, but what can be observed is the building of respectable and probably well-run public houses. Very often these were also of greater architectural pretensions than either the town's old inns or its beer houses, although some inns, like the Talbot mentioned earlier, had been rebuilt in impressive styles. Another of these is the Star in Westgate, rebuilt in 1896 for Hammonds Brewery to become the New Star Inn (5.15). Built of ashlar, it has been designed in a somewhat austere classical style, but with scrolled baroque pediments adding some relief to the ground-floor entrances, the first-floor windows having thin pediments, although the building was originally designed with a domed lantern above the eaves on the corner. There were also new public houses such as the Belle Vue, Manningham (5.16), which has a rather French air with its Mansard roof and high dormer windows together with a chateau-like tower.

This chapter began with St George's Hall, and described it as a significant building in that it marked the beginning of an attempt to instil a spirit of civic pride as well as provide a decent alternative place of entertainment to drinking and carousing. There

5.15 The Star, Westgate, Bradford, 1896, Samuel Jackson & Son.

5.16 The Belle Vue, Manningham Lane, Manningham, 1874.

were other theatres and places of cultural entertainment, but these have been lost either through demolition or disasters like fires – the Theatre Royal in Manningham Lane was one, for example. But there are two others. One is Cartwright Hall (5.17), the city's first art gallery, built in Lister Park in 1904. The first thoughts of Bradford councillors on this subject was to build a museum of technology, but a museum of the arts together with a suite of public rooms was the proposal that was

5.17 Cartwright Hall, Manningham, 1904, Simpson and Allen.

5.18 The Alhambra Theatre, Bradford, 1914, Chadwick and Watson.

put out to architectural competition. It was won by the London firm of Simpson and Allen who produced a huge baroque assemblage of building rising from a heavily rusticated base and culminating in a Vanbrugh-like cupola.

The other building is the Alhambra Theatre (5.18) situated in the centre of Bradford. It was built in 1914 by Francis Laidler, a music hall entrepreneur, who owned a further two music halls in the city. The Alhambra, however, was perhaps the most lavish of these. Despite its name it has little to do with Spain or the Moors, and its architects described it as 'English renaissance of the Georgian period'[3]. However one may wish to categorise this, it demonstrates that popular entertainment had come a long way since the 1840s, and these two buildings represent the culminating point of half a century's endeavour to reform the cultural life of Bradford through both private and public enterprise.

Religion and Education

Religion and education were further channels along which an ethic of respectability flowed. Spiritual leaders and commentators viewed industrial towns and cities swollen by a rapid influx of people as places where irreligion might flourish as traditional values and social bonds broke down. Yet how were people expected to maintain religious practice when the number of places of worship did not keep pace with the rising population? It was partly for this reason and partly because of competition between faiths that a great number of churches were built.

The Bradford Church Building Society was formed in 1859 with the goal of building ten new Anglican churches in the borough, a goal that was achieved by 1872. The outstanding church of this group is All Saints, Little Horton Green (5.19) built in 1864. The site was given by Francis Sharp Powell of Horton Old Hall, a landowner, lawyer and MP, who also paid for the church's construction. Externally, it is the tower and spire that arrest the attention.

Placed to one side of the body of the church, it gives a massive vertical accent to the grouping and is a landmark that can be recognised from many parts of the city. It has been designed in a Decorated style of Gothic, but draws on France for its influence also.

5.19 All Saints, Little Horton Green, Little Horton, 1864, T.H. and F. Healey.

5.20 Great Horton Methodist Church, Great Horton Road, Great Horton, 1861-63, Samuel Jackson.

Nonconformist faiths were also responsible for a good deal of building in the city. Unlike Anglican churches, the architecture of nonconformity is usually Italianate rather than Gothic, particularly the Methodist chapels of which there are some fine examples in Bradford. One of the most pleasing is Great Horton Methodist Church (5.20) completed in 1863 which even at this late date retains a Palladian feel in its proportions and temple front; but it is also true to its time in the detailing of the window surrounds and doorways.

Southend Hall (5.21) also continues this design tradition in its arch-headed windows, arranged here almost like arcades, and their exaggerated keystones, although it was designed and built between 1878-1880.

Some nonconformist chapels were designed in Gothic styles, however, and the Annesley Methodist Chapel (5.22) in Little Horton Lane is one example. Built in 1865, it is almost contemporaneous with the building of All Saints Church a little further up the road, and stands in its shadow somewhat. It also has a similar massing to All Saints – if smaller in scale – in the placing of its spire to one side of the main range. Perhaps the most striking feature is the large geometric tracery head of its east window.

Anglicanism and nonconformity were the predominant faiths of the district until the beginning of the nineteenth century. But immigration throughout the century brought culture groups of different religious persuasions. The largest of these groups were the Irish who were largely Catholic. St Patrick's Church (5.23) in Westgate was located in one of the chief areas of Irish settlement in Bradford. Built in 1853 it is in a simple, but dignified Gothic Revival style with a pencil-thin belfry. To the

5.21 Southend Hall, Tickhill Street, Leeds Road, Bradford, 1880, George Ogden.

5.22 Annesley Methodist Chapel, Little Horton Lane, 1865, Andrews & Pepper.

left is the presbytery, a more elaborate Gothic with an oriel bay window and a French-looking assemblage of roofs.

The Irish were not the only migrant group. Scottish Presbyterians built St Andrew's Presbyterian Church also in Westgate in 1849, while German immigrants built the Deutsche Evangelische Kirke in Great Horton Road. German Jewish immigrants were to build the first synagogues in Bradford. The Bowland Street Reformed Synagogue (5.24) was built in 1880, and is a small but slightly exotic design by Francis Healey employing red sandstone banding and decorative arched heads to the openings in a style that was known at the time as Saracenic.

Education might seem like an unusual subject to bracket with religion, but until 1870 there were three means to obtaining a primary education, one of these being

5.23 *Above:* St Patrick's, Westgate, Bradford, 1853, Weightman, Hadfield and Goldie.

5.24 *Left:* Jewish Reformed Synagogue, Bowland Street, Manningham, 1880, Francis Healey.

church schools, the others being private schools and factory schools. The Church of England was a prolific builder of schools in nineteenth-century Bradford. The Parochial Schools Fund had been established by the Revd Dr Scoresby shortly after he had been appointed vicar of Bradford in 1839. Scoresby's idea was that every parish should have a church school, and between 1839 and 1846 nine parochial schools had been built; the process did not end there, further schools were built by his successor John Burnett. The parish church's own school was originally built in 1841, but was replaced by a larger school (5.25) in 1871. The style is a simple Gothic with accommodation organised along a front range which has projecting rear wings. The nonconformists were also active in building schools. A good example is the Congregationalist school in Great Horton Road (5.26). This was built in 1868

5.25 *Above left:* The Parish Church School, Captain Street, 1871, Samuel Jackson.

5.26 *Above right:* Congregationalist School, Great Horton Road, Great Horton, 1868, Paul and Robinson.

5.27 *Right:* Barkerend School, Hendon Drive, Bradford, 1874, Andrews & Pepper.

to the designs of the Manchester firm Paul and Robinson who produce a rugged, no-nonsense Gothic design complete with bell tower and an unusual tripartite window in the gable.

But this was built on the eve of a great revolution in education. Forster's Education Act came into force in 1870 giving rise to state schooling through locally funded Board Schools. While some Anglican schools remained church schools, most of the nonconformist schools had closed by the end of the century. Forster was a Bradford MP, and the town responded to his Act with plans to build a number of Board Schools almost immediately. In fact the architecture of this first wave of school building in Bradford produced some of the most lavish schools seen in the city then or now. The leading architectural firms were commissioned to design schools in different parts of the borough and Barkerend Board School (5.27) is the design by Andrews & Pepper. Built in 1874, the school has entrances for boys and girls at either end of a range that contains the hall and classrooms. While these rooms are lit by unexceptional cusped windows, the striking feature of the design is a pair of return gables that rise through two storeys to accommodate large arched windows that contain elaborate plate tracery. The long sloping roof and features such as the cluster of stone chimneys (one set missing, far left) add further interest to the profile.

The Bradford School Board was also quick to experiment with Higher Grade Schools. Indeed, the Bradford Board was the first in the country to provide a system of Higher Grade Schools where boys *and* girls – often from better-off families – could be educated from elementary to secondary level in subjects that went beyond the standard curriculum of reading, writing and mathematics. The Belle Vue Schools (5.28) for boys and girls had been opened in 1877, but were to be expanded and rebuilt in 1895 in a Renaissance style by the architects Hargreaves and Bailey. The frontage building in Manningham Lane shown here proudly displays the legend 'Bradford School Board, Belle Vue Higher Boys' School'. The school extends to the rear eventually reaching Lumb Lane and the Higher Girls' School which is located there.

The development of education in nineteenth-century Bradford also extended to technical and further education. In 1832 a Mechanics' Institute was formed. Then in the 1850s a college to further education in art, design and technology was proposed, although the proposal remained only that for nearly thirty years before any such scheme came to a final result. Eventually the Bradford Technical School was built on a site in Great Horton Road and opened in 1883. The new Technical School (5.29) was designed by Hope and Jardine and won great praise in its day – the *London Magazine* described it as 'a building on a scale of completeness which will throw into the shade any previous attempts made in this direction in the country.'[4] Magnificent classical building though it is with a stunning entrance – a giant doorcase surmounted by a baroque tower – yet few other than Pevsner have asked why the range to the right of the entrance has columns along its exterior, while that to the left has pilasters? It is very odd.

5.28 Belle Vue Higher Grade Schools, Manningham Lane, 1895, Hargreaves and Bailey.

5.29 Bradford Technical School, Great Horton Road, 1882, Hope and Jardine.

Industrial Buildings

The last chapter stated that while a number of Bradford's first textile mills were large mills with a modicum of architectural embellishment, most early mills were, nevertheless, small buildings lacking any architectural pretensions. It is my opinion that a turning point came in the Bradford district with the building of Saltaire Mills between 1851 and 1853. Titus Salt is credited with the pioneering of 'alpaca Orleans' or lustre cloths and by 1850 was conducting his business from a number of mills in Bradford. Wishing to consolidate this business as well as provide a model industrial village where social and moral health could be maintained, he acquired a site in rural surroundings three miles to the north of Bradford in Shipley. Here he set about building the mill and industrial village which has become internationally famous. The mill was important in two respects. Firstly, it was among the first truly integrated worsted mills (all processes under one roof) in the district; secondly, it was designed with a level of architectural enrichment to which no other mills in Bradford up to that date had aspired. This, together with their huge scale, set a precedent locally. Saltaire Mills (5.30) were designed in an Italianate style by Lockwood & Mawson. Nowhere had this Italianate detailing of round-headed windows, pediments, eaves cornices and towers with campanili been applied to the architecture of a mill with quite such thoroughness. Even the chimney, after rising from a podium, terminated in a great cluster of acanthus leaves (removed in the 1970s). It is not going too far to say that it was probably Salt and this mill that gave both the exemplar and the invitation for others to follow.

5.30 Saltaire Mills, Victoria Road, Saltaire, 1853, Lockwood & Mawson.

5.31 Whetley Mills, Thornton Road, 1863, Milnes & France.

5.32 Brigella Mills, Little Horton Lane, 1871 and later.

Other textile firms did follow this lead. Daniel Illingworth & Sons' Whetley Mills (5.31) is one example. Although not so through-going in its detailing as Saltaire Mills, its heroic scale and the grouping of its buildings in a long perspective along Thornton Road remains impressive, as does the mill chimney. Illingworth's was a combing and spinning mill. Others were built as integrated mills, combing, spinning and manufacturing cloth. Brigella Mills in Little Horton Lane were rebuilt around 1871 for J. Briggs & Company, and display the typical buildings of the worsted mill (5.32). In front is a long single-storeyed building, probably combing and weaving sheds; to the left, the spinning mill; to the right, warehousing and offices whose frontage to Little Horton Lane has been designed in an Italianate style. All of this seems to have been organised around the power plant, indicated by the tall chimney that rises from a podium.

It would be a mistake to think that all textile mills built in Bradford in the nineteenth century were worsted mills. The grandest of them all, Manningham Mills (5.33), was rebuilt as a silk mill in 1873 after a fire had destroyed an earlier mill on the site. Samuel Cunliffe-Lister, later Baron Masham, could be said to have had three careers in the

5.33 *Above Left:* Manningham Mills, Heaton Road, Manningham, 1873, Andrews & Pepper.

5.34 *Above right:* Manningham Mills: detail of the Heaton Road entrance.

5.35 *Left:* Oakwood Dye Works, City Road, Bradford, 1873.

5.36 *Below:* Legrams Mill, Legrams Lane, Bradford, 1873.

textile industry: in perfecting and marketing his machine wool comb; in recovering and spinning silk from silk waste; and in the application of power weaving to plush manufacture. Manningham Mills, built high on the side of the North Beck Valley, is a landmark that can be seen from many parts of Bradford. Its chimney is modelled on a northern Italian bell tower and is panelled in a similar way to that in St Mark's Square in Venice, while the mill buildings themselves blend Italian and French classical design in this truly monumental industrial building. The Heaton Road entrance (5.34) is particularly eye-catching with an almost Romanesque arched doorway set within a more conventionally classical frame. Above the doorway are the arms and motto not of Cunliffe nor Lister, but Kaye, another family with which the Cunliffes had married.

While there were many other industries in Bradford – ironworks, for example – the predominant one was textiles. Also, other industries were textile related – Oakwood Dye Works, City Road, for instance, which developed into a huge complex, mostly after 1873, taking in cotton goods for dyeing. Now only the entrance (5.35) and a truncated range of building survives. However, the entrance that remains hints at the scale of the original complex, and the bell tower with its sandstone louvres is a dramatic feature.

Textile machine making was another related industry of which there are few remains now. Legrams Mill in Legrams Lane still dominates this area of the city (5.36). Built in 1873, it is uncertain whether it was intended for textile production, but it was operating as a loom-making works for the last twenty-five years of the century in the ownership of George Hodgson who in 1893 was described as 'the most extensive maker of looms in the United Kingdom.'[5] It was later acquired by a Keighley firm who converted it to worsted spinning.

Houses

Much was made in the previous chapter of the sharp rise in population in the first half of the century. Although the rate of population increase declined in the second half of the century, numbers continued to grow, nevertheless. In 1851 the population of the borough stood at 103,771, yet in 1881 it was 183,032. While this figure included the township of Bolton which had become part of the borough through a boundary change, Bolton's population accounted for only 2,573. The point is that all these people had to be housed. As we have seen, the typical house type for working-class occupation was the terrace of back-to-back cottages, possibly with a cellar dwelling beneath. There were good reasons for condemning much of this housing – damp, poorly built, inadequate sanitation, lack of a pure water supply – but the over-riding criticism was of the house type itself. The newly formed Bradford Council monitored back-to-back house building with vigour through its Building Committee which reported in 1854 on 'the continued practice of building houses back-to-back. Out of 1,401 sanctioned, 1,071 or 76.9 per cent are laid out upon that objectionable principle.'[6] This illustrates two things: the large numbers of back-to-backs being built; and the very high percentage of total numbers built that were back-to-back. In 1860 the council acted to put a halt to this by passing a bye-law that required free space to two sides of any house built. In effect this put a stop to the building of the worst of the back-to-back terraces. But it caused uproar. Many builders, speculators and building clubs complained of the restraints and costs that this put on their activities. And it was an issue that would not go away. Matters came to a head in the election of 1865 when the chairman of the Building Committee lost his seat. By the end of 1865 the bye-law was reformed, and back-to-back house building resumed, but subject to new regulations: between every pair of houses there had to be a wide passageway; cellar dwellings were banned, as were enclosed courts of back-to-backs.

This gave rise to a distinctive form of Bradford house, the 'tunnel back'. Gaythorne Street (5.37), Great Horton provides a good example. Built between 1872 and 1873 as the speculation of William Casson, a butcher, these houses have accommodation on two floors with two rooms to each floor. On the ground floor are the principal living room and a scullery. The back houses are laid out on the same plan and so are the adjoining houses which are separated from each other by a wide passage. In the rear yard are four privies, two for every pair of houses. Ward Street (5.38), also in Great Horton, illustrates more back-to-back housing, but here the accommodation is ungenerous – there is no separate scullery, just one room on the ground floor with a sink at the cellar head. Again all the privies are located in a yard to the rear. Although some of this housing offered better accommodation, both spatially and in terms of sanitation, it was hardly luxurious. Housing such as this was developed piecemeal by speculation over a couple of years.

Entrepreneurs, too, played a part in the reform of working-class housing. There were grand designs for model industrial communities in Bradford, such as Ripleyville,

5.37 Gaythorne Street, Great Horton, 1873.

5.38 Ward Street, Great Horton, 1872-74, Ephraim Watmough.

the creation of Henry Ripley of the Bowling Dye Works. This was an urban village containing not only houses, but also a church and school. The site has now been cleared, unlike Rand Street (5.39). This is hardly a model industrial village, but a street of houses built for William Rand, one of Bradford's earlier generation of textile entrepreneurs. Their purpose, as the plan states, was to provide 'twenty improved dwelling houses for working men.'[7] The street has been designed with simple Gothic detail which lifts them above the ordinary, while the ground floor contains an entrance hall and two rooms; there are two rooms upstairs, a small attic and a wash-cellar. This represented good accommodation in terms of working-class housing. The houses were completed shortly after Rand's death in 1866, and it is clear from the census and trade directories that the houses were not occupied by 'working men', but the lower middle class – managers, travelling salesmen or small shopkeepers, for example.

Historians have sometimes overlooked housing improvement of a different kind. By this I do not mean the working-class building clubs which might build appalling houses as a speculation, but the houses built by co-operative societies, largely in the later nineteenth century. Such housing was usually built to decent standards for members and others, and it demonstrates more of a democratic attitude to improvement rather than speculation or paternalistic reform. Leamington Street (5.40), Manningham, was built by the Bradford Provident Industrial Society in 1892. If simply detailed, it was well built and had good sanitary provision and accommodation. It had been built on land acquired earlier in the century which was developed with other streets of small terraces – Victor Terrace and Victor Street were further co-operative housing developments providing houses for both working- and lower middle-class families.

Although these houses were built in Manningham and were working-class/ lower middle-class housing, the overwhelming development and character of Manningham was as a middle-class suburb, and it might be viewed as the top

5.39 Rand Street, Great Horton, 1866, John Simpson.

5.40 Leamington Street, Manningham, 1892, Ryecroft and Firth.

suburb of nineteenth-century Bradford. Some Manningham houses have already been mentioned in the previous chapter, such as the neo-classical terraces on Manningham Lane. But after 1850 this suburb was developed with different house types – detached and semi-detached villas as well terraces, and designed in both Italianate and Gothic Revival styles. Italianate designs can be found from the 1850s. Clifton House (5.41) was designed by Andrews and Delauney for Jacob Philipp, a German merchant, in 1851. It is a house that still has a neo-classical feel to it, but shades into the Italianate with detailing such as its overhanging eaves. Peel Square (5.42), on the other hand, is a terrace built for the Crown Building Society in 1854,

5.41 *Right:* Clifton House, Clifton Place, Manningham, 1851, Andrews and Delauney.

5.42 *Below:* Peel Square, Lumb Lane, 1854, William Metcalfe (?).

possibly the architect William Metcalfe, who was one of the trustees of the Society. Its striking feature is the bold central pediment set within a generally well-proportioned arrangement of houses in more of a terrace than a square. But the finest of the Italianate terraces is Samuel Jackson's Blenheim Mount (5.43) of 1865. Three storeys in height, it supplies palatial accommodation in terraced form combining some decidedly French-looking detailing with the Italian, especially in the centre.

While Italianate designs were popular until the 1870s and beyond, Gothic Revival styles had been introduced by the 1840s; and by the 1850s and '60s, Bradford architects had become practised in supplying both Italianate and Gothic designs for their clients.

5.43 Blenheim Mount, Manningham Lane, Manningham, 1865, Samuel Jackson.

5.44 Mount Royd, Park Road, Manningham, 1863, Lockwood & Mawson (?).

Mount Royd (5.44) is a series of semi-detached villas, each pair in alternate Gothic and Italianate designs and thought to be by Lockwood & Mawson. Like Blenheim Mount across the road, these are tall and spacious houses offering the sort of accommodation that the most successful of Bradford's professional and mercantile middle class desired.

Gothic detail was applied to some more modest houses, also, such as Devonshire Terrace (5.45) where the basic model for a terrace has been given a Gothic feel by the addition of uncomplicated pointed arches to windows and doorways.

More elaborate Gothic designs can be found in Manningham as they can in Bradford's other suburb, Little Horton. The detailing of a large terrace in Lower Ashgrove (5.46) by Thomas Campbell Hope is a good example of the sorts of

5.45 Devonshire Terrace, St Mary's Road, Manningham, *c.* 1850.

5.46 Detail of houses in Lower Ashgrove, Little Horton, 1874, Thomas Campbell Hope.

5.47 Two houses in St Paul's Road, Manningham, 1891, Herbert Issit.

5.48 The grave stele of the Robertshaw family in Undercliffe Cemetery, the great necropolis overlooking Bradford.

embellishment that can be found in some of Bradford's nineteenth-century houses, local sandstones supplying an excellent material for the masons to work.

Gothic and Italianate styles dominated architectural design for most of the second half of the nineteenth century, but later in the century, from perhaps the 1880s, styles influenced by the Arts and Crafts Movement and some classically derived styles came to prominence. The two houses in St Paul's Road (5.47), Manningham, are a good example of a style termed by contemporaries 'Queen Anne'. They were built to the designs of Herbert Issit in 1891 for J. Craven, and combine a traditional Elizabethan Gothic with classical elements such as the triangular pediments above the gables. They were amongst the last of the grand houses built in Manningham.

Conclusion

In 1897 Bradford was granted city status. This was the final accolade bestowed on the city, and it was conferred not simply because the town had expanded greatly in size, but because of its industrial and commercial importance. Its Town Hall became the place where the business of a city was to be transacted, and as we have already seen it was to be enlarged by that doyen of the nineteenth-century architectural profession, Richard Norman Shaw. Yet while Bradford in the 1890s may appear to have been the epitome of a successful industrial city, it could also be argued that it was already past its peak – there had been a serious trade depression in the mid-1870s and in the 1880s and '90s there was increasing foreign competition. While it would be wrong to argue for a continuum of decline from the late '70s, nevertheless, the glory days of the middle decades of the century were over.

6 FROM MODERNISM TO POSTMODERNISM: TWENTIETH-CENTURY BRADFORD

Introduction

'Modern' and 'postmodern' are words commonly used, but rarely with precision. Before I go any further, I want to say what I mean by these words, since they occur in the title of this chapter, and they need to be defined in terms of how I am going to use them when applied to architecture. Modern or modernism are the words that probably most people feel at home with. Modern can be said to mean contemporary, up-to-date, perhaps a little in advance of its time, even. These sorts of meanings have attached themselves to the word, but modern is a word that can be used in more precise ways, too. When we apply it to architecture its more specific meaning implies a building that conforms to the architectural principles of the International Modern Movement. International Modern, Modern Movement or Modernism rose to prominence in Europe and the USA between 1900 and 1940. It was a revolution in design that largely rejected past precedents and favoured designs of cubic form using building materials in new and creative ways. Concrete or Portland stone might be used to clad steel-framed structures built to modern designs. But modernism was more than this: it was an ideology also, that advocated vigorous change and such change was characterised as progress, seen as a desirable objective in itself. If this architecture and ideology made an impact in Europe between the wars, it made less of one in Britain. It was not until the post-war years that modernism became the defining style in the reconstruction of Britain's towns and cities in the 1950s, '60s and early '70s.

There were, of course, modernist architects working in Britain between the wars, and to read some accounts of the history of twentieth-century architecture, one might be tempted to believe that modernism was the only style, but it was not. The architectural history of the twentieth century is much more complex, and to understand why modernism did not become predominant until after 1945 it is necessary to understand something of this history. To begin with there was a lingering Gothic or vernacular tradition that was surprisingly long lived. It was a line of development that led from the Arts and Crafts architecture of the 1880s and continued to influence design in the use of traditional forms of detail and construction until the 1930s and even after. At the same time classical architecture remained an important design source. Houses in classical styles are rare in this period, but architects of public and some industrial buildings still relied on the classical for inspiration. These were either as reinterpretations of eighteenth-century classicism (sometimes referred to as Wrenaissance); or a spare form of classicism reduced to its basic elements – stripped classicism. None of this should come as a revelation. A number of architects who had been working in late Victorian and Edwardian times were still in practice up until the 1930s or even 1940s – the great figure here is Sir Edwin Lutyens. Also a generation of architects at the beginning of the twentieth century were trained in offices or were taught at schools of architecture where many of the staff were themselves the products of the Victorian system of architectural education, and whose outlook was rooted in these traditions.

It is hardly surprising that it was not until the post-war years and more particularly from about the 1960s to the 1980s that modernism predominated. It developed, too, from early experiments with cubic forms to high-rise structures of steel, glass and stone cladding; to systems building where large sections were manufactured for assembly on site; to what was probably the lowest point to which British architecture has sunk in the unadorned and bleak concrete finishes of some buildings – 'brutalism', as it has been labelled.

Enter the postmodern. This term can be defined in a number of different ways, but architecturally it is a rejection of the modern. By the 1980s the future of modernism was being called into question. First of all there were the structural failures of this type of architecture, but more importantly a new generation began to reappraise the recent past and to question the concept of progress. Inflation, mass unemployment, social unrest, or the sink estates that many cities had acquired by the '80s did not sit well with the idea of progress embodied in modernist ideology. Postmodernism arose against this background. Postmodern architecture is a part of this – it is the acceptance of modern building techniques and materials, but its design makes reference to past forms of architecture and freely interprets these in a variety of ways. Yet if postmodernism was in the driving seat in the 1990s, the modernists did not go away and had much to learn from postmodern architecture, especially in the ways in which it exploited the different qualities of building materials. At the beginning of the twenty-first century, modernism is making something of a comeback, but in new ways – neo-modernism as it might be called.

Aside from architecture, we might also think of the twentieth century as modern in the ways in which we have developed distinctive institutions and technologies. The welfare state, telecommunications, or the predominance of the motorcar are all manifestations of the modern. It is around these sorts of subjects that the discussion of the architecture of Bradford in the twentieth century is organized in the following pages, for what was distinctive about Bradford's industry, housing or public buildings in the nineteenth century started to disappear in the twentieth as mass communications and internationalism in architecture began to erode the local.

THE BEGINNINGS OF THE MODERN: 1900-1945

Housing

Moves towards the above conception of the modern can be seen in Bradford from the late nineteenth century in the council's response to the mass of slum housing in the city. The Longlands district of Bradford on the edge of the city centre had long been regarded as the worst area of housing. In 1870, for example, the journalist James Burnley had exposed conditions there as a disgrace.[1] But it was not until the end of the century that something could be done about it, for while legislation that permitted slum clearance existed, councils were under no obligation to re-house the occupiers of the houses to be demolished, simply to compensate the owners. The Housing of the Working Classes Act of 1890 changed that situation by allowing councils to build housing subsidised by the rates. Following this Act left-wing members of Bradford Council proposed a clearing of Longlands and replacing it with municipally owned housing. This proposal was opposed by right-wing elements and also the Catholic Church which, in this mostly Irish quarter of the city, saw a threat of its congregation's being dispersed. The scheme was nevertheless carried through. By 1904 a number of houses were built in Faxfleet Street, Wibsey, now a part of the expanded borough, and over the next ten years further houses were added. When Longlands itself was cleared, the council began to construct its first tenement blocks or flats which were completed in 1909, further blocks following in 1910. These flats were decently built and had a little decorative detailing to enliven their frontages. At Roundhill Place (6.1) half-timbering of the gables and light iron railings to the balconies have been used in a modest two-storey row of tenements.

Bradford Council continued to add to its stock of housing over the next thirty years with an expansion of housing in the first area of municipally owned housing at Wibsey, for example, and in the building of estates closer to the city centre in the old borough townships such as the Canterbury Avenue estate in Horton mostly in the late 1930s.

However, the council was not the only provider of working-class housing. While it is true to say that some speculative building continued and older housing was

6.1 *Left:* Roundhill Place, Bradford, 1909-10, Bradford Council.

6.2 *Below:* Housing provided by the Sutton Trust, Sutton Road, 1930s, Chorley, Gibbon and Frogett.

improved, charitable trusts also supplied housing sometimes creating model estates. The Sutton Trust is one example building houses in several parts of the country, including Bradford. The Sutton Trust's estate in Bradford (6.2) is located on what was a piece of open ground along Dick Lane in Tyersal. It was built between 1931 and 1938 and could be seen as a small garden suburb, since here was an attempt to build more than simply houses. When completed it comprised 221 houses and eighty-seven flats which were arranged in small groupings in low densities and along a sweeping crescent looking out onto green public spaces, in the centre of which was a community hall. There were also tennis courts and play areas.[2]

Industry and Commerce

To write about industry and commerce in the interwar years is to write about boom and bust. Immediately after the First World War Bradford's textile industry flourished in response to a world demand for textiles, but by the late 1920s a depression had set in that lasted into the 1930s during which time many businesses disappeared. Nevertheless, Bradford remained a centre for the trade in wool and textiles and factories and warehouses continued to be built. The massive warehouses illustrated (6.3) stand in Bolton Road and were built in 1912 to the designs of James Ledingham largely as wool and yarn warehousing. While unmistakably of the first quarter of the twentieth century, they also show some of the influence of the earlier Queen Anne style especially in their entrances, hardly surprising given that Ledingham had trained in the later nineteenth century. Yet they prefigure the sort of classicism that was to become prevalent in the 1930s. They continue, indeed, an indomitable classical tradition, their arcaded fronts supported on giant pilasters which rise from a rusticated sandstone base, although they are also moving away from earlier origins in the use of non-traditional materials: the walling of their upper storeys is faced with white tile. They occupy a transitional position in the architecture of the city.

6.3 Warehouse, Bolton Road, Bradford, 1912, James Ledingham.

Pure examples of a stripped classical style began to appear in Bradford in the 1930s. The telephone exchange (6.4) is a good example. This was built in 1938 to deal with Bradford's growing telecommunications system. At first its clean lines, flat roofline and the whiteness of its Portland stone walls suggest a modernist design, but a closer look reveals a rusticated base with an unembellished classical doorcase. On this base the main body of the building is supported containing windows that are similarly unadorned except for the bronze panels between the floors. It is a sleekly designed exchange perhaps symbolising the technological sophistication of urban life: it is a noticeable feature of buildings of the General Post Office between the wars that in the country or in small towns they tended to be designed in vernacular styles using local materials.

Classicism is also present in the design of some factories. The small spinning mill built for Bernhard Gosling on the corners of Barnard Road, Rhine Street and Rutland Street in Bowling (6.5) is an example now probably unique in Bradford, if somewhat dilapidated. It was built in 1922 with classical detail stripped down to basic elements such as pilasters, bands and simple cornices. At the same time it seems to look forward to the modern in its massing – the way cubic forms are juxtaposed – and in the large amount of wall space given over to glass. So far the architect of this rather interesting and early classical/modernist design has evaded research, but it suggests a familiarity with the work of some German architects both before and after the First World War.

Modernist designs of buildings can be found in Bradford more typically from the 1930s. Probably the largest modernist building in the city then was the Co-operative

6.4 The Telephone Exchange, Manchester Road, Bradford, 1938, General Post Office.

Society's Sunwin House (6.6). The Society had had premises on a site on the corner of Godwin Street and Sunbridge Road since the end of the nineteenth century, but, architecturally, these premises were to be revolutionised by the complete rebuilding of the store in 1935 to the designs of W.A. Johnson. Sunwin House stands on a steeply sloping site to which the design has been well adapted. The principal front on

6.5 *Above:* Bernhard Gosling's worsted spinning factory, 1922.

6.6 *Right:* Sunwin House, Sunbridge Road, Bradford, 1935, W.A. Johnson.

Sunbridge Road is a long display front terminated by towers at either end containing the staircases and entrances. These are in effect the most prominent features, being tall cylinders and one of which forms a stop to the vista along Kirkgate.

Entertainment

A major form of entertainment remained the public house, and Bradford had no shortage of these; nor did it have a shortage of brewers. The Melbourne Brewery was one that also owned and built pubs in the interwar years. The Melbourne Arms, White Abbey Road (6.7), was one such, built in 1935. It is typical of the period with a stylised classical front and entrance, the whole being clad in polychrome tile.

However, the newest form of entertainment, and the one that was growing the fastest, was the cinema. The Picture Palace (6.8) was opened at Dudley Hill in 1912 for Goodhall's Pictures Ltd. Like many small early cinemas the design was unsophisticated: unadorned sides and a rear lacking windows (the need to exclude light), but a fancy frontage. The Picture Palace is built of brick and has detailing in white tile to the main front which is an elaborate classical design with a pediment supported on brick and tile pilasters that frame the main entrance – a palace of popular entertainment of the most up-to-date sort.

But the most imposing of Bradford's cinemas was that which has become known as the Odeon (6.9). Designed by William Illingworth in 1930 it opened as the New Victoria, a combination of ballroom, café and cinema with a seating capacity of

6.7 The Melbourne Arms, White Abbey Road, 1935, W.A. Johnson.

above 3,000. It is a massive landmark in central Bradford. Plain brick is again used for the walling material, but it is enlivened by classical detailing in tile and the two great classical entrance towers add a solidity and grandeur and are similarly detailed in white tile – pilasters, round-headed windows with keystones and domes. Was this twin-towered form perhaps an inspiration for Johnson when he designed Sunwin House five years later? And had the twin towers of the earlier Alhambra Theatre been an inspiration for Illingworth? It is difficult to say. At the time of writing something of a question mark hangs over the future of the Odeon.

6.8 *Right:* The Picture Palace, Dudley Hill, 1912, Howorth & Howorth.

6.9 *Below:* The Odeon, Prince's Way, 1930, William Illingworth..

DESTRUCTION AND RECONSTRUCTION: CENTRAL BRADFORD 1945-2005

The first forty years of the twentieth century in Bradford saw different approaches to architectural design, no one of them gaining a predominance. But by the 1950s and until the 1980s there was really only one style – modernism. Progressivist notions about the future of society after the Second World War and the war damage that had been inflicted on some cities led to a position where metaphor and reality met in terms such as 'rebuilding'. Implicit in the physical rebuilding of our towns and cities was the notion of rebuilding the civic and moral fibre of urban society. As one author put it towards the end of the war when writing about town planning: 'The folly of the last century must go, the chaos, the slums and the dirt; so also, the crimes of our own century, the mock-Tudor suburbs, the ribbon-development and the imitation Classic.'[3] Here was the cry of the modernist planner, and similar sentiments were expressed up and down the country including in Bradford.

The genesis of the redevelopment of central Bradford in the 1960s, together with the reaction to it, has already been outlined in Chapter 1 (see pages 28-9). When completed in the late 1960s, Bradford had become transformed. Regrets had been expressed and protests had been made against the loss of landmark buildings, buildings which, if demolished in the 1960s and '70s, continue to be held in affection by a generation that grew up with them – Swan Arcade, Exchange Station, Kirkgate Market, or the Mechanics' Institute. These and other buildings in the town were swept away to make room for offices and retail space of different kinds. The latest casualty in this architectural cleansing of the city was Kirkgate Market, a large covered market of 1871 designed by Lockwood & Mawson. In its place arose the insipidly named Kirkgate Centre, concrete brutalism of nearly a hundred years on, its joyless exterior bulking large on Darley Street in the main shopping area, its entrances, especially those on Kirkgate and Westgate, lacking impact. This was to be matched in brutality by High Point the former headquarters of the Yorkshire Building Society (6.10). This was again a raw concrete tower, the sections of its sides cast in a hard corrugated texture. Like the Kirkgate Centre its entrance has little presence, and does not invite. The turbulence created by this tall building produces what seems like a ceaseless wind along New John Street.

But the '60s was not all bad news. There were also some buildings of quality. Central Library (6.11) designed by the city architect W.C. Brown and opened in 1967 is one. In conception it is undoubtedly modern, yet almost classical in its form – a tower clad in Portland stone that is mounted on a raw slate plinth. In this respect it looks back to the rustication of plinths and bases found in many classical buildings.

The original design incorporated not only a large library on several floors with remarkable views across the city, but also a theatre, an art gallery and a café, services and cultural features that have mostly disappeared now: only the library remains. However, in terms of cultural and educational innovation the institution

6.10 High Point, Westgate, Bradford.

6.11 Central Library, Prince's Way, Bradford, 1967, W.C. Brown.

that has contributed greatly to the city came in 1966 under the expansion of higher education by the Wilson government. Bradford's College of Advanced Technology was granted university status and opened by Wilson himself who was chancellor of the university for many years. The principal entrance is the Richmond Building (6.12), a typical and unremarkable modernist conception in its main building, but with a deep portico that houses one of the university's lecture theatres above. At the time of writing the campus is undergoing a complete refurbishment.

Bradford in the 1960s was not simply a city of architectural change. All of the changes to the city centre were planned in conjunction with a new road system and connection to a motorway. This led to the widening of some roads out of the city, and along the Manchester and Wakefield roads, this went hand-in-hand with the clearance of much poor-quality housing on either side. The result, however, was far from satisfactory with areas of the city divided by, in places, six-lane highways and the provision of tower block accommodation (6.13). In order to cross roads like these, bridges were provided to housing on opposite sides of the road; or subways (6.14) which were a common way of getting across city centre roads also. Most bridges and some subways are now being eliminated, but it seems likely that there will be no alternative to others.

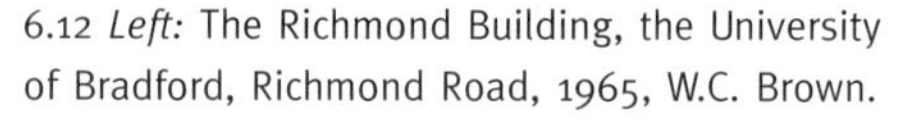

6.12 *Left:* The Richmond Building, the University of Bradford, Richmond Road, 1965, W.C. Brown.

6.13 *Below left:* New developments of the 1960s and '70s in Manchester Road.

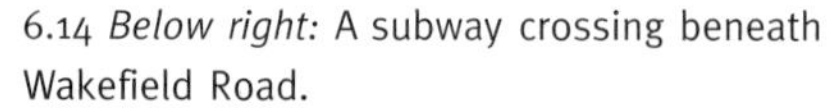

6.14 *Below right:* A subway crossing beneath Wakefield Road.

DOUBTS AND FAITH 1980-2005

The problems with modernist planning and architecture were becoming evident by the late 1960s and '70s. Some significant failures – Ronan Point, 1968, for instance – the problems of living in tower blocks and the problems caused by monstrous roads can be seen as specific architectural or planning problems. But by the late 1970s and '80s modernist conceptions of the progressive had also been brought into question. Doubts, rather than the certainty of progress, characterised the *post*modern. As stated above, the word postmodern will be used in this chapter to mean, architecturally, a period after the modern in which modern building techniques are used, but in designs that often mimic or reinvent the past styles; or which make witty plays on the differences between the textures or strengths of materials – glass and stone, say.

One of the more accomplished postmodern buildings of Bradford is one that many people are perhaps unaware of. This is the Unity Building (6.15) at the School of Health Studies, a part of the University of Bradford, on Trinity Road, Little Horton. This new block closes an earlier open quadrangle of building and makes reference in its design to neo-classical buildings of the eighteenth or nineteenth centuries – the symmetrical front with a semi-circular or cylindrical entrance and semi-circular projections from the ends of the building relate to such sources. The contrast of materials in its walling – brick rising from a stone plinth and stone banding – also add to this impression.

The office building illustrated at 6.16 stands on part of the site of the former Forster Square Railway Station and was built in the 1990s also. There is perhaps a

6.15. The Unity Building, School of Health Studies, Trinity Road, 1994. J.H. Langtry-Langton Partners.

6.16 Offices on the Forster Square Station site.

6.17 Centenary Square, new leisure and shopping, 2004.

6.18 Darfield Street Mosque, largely 1990s.

reflection of the former use of this site in the roofline of the building. Although the segmental profile of roofs became common in the architecture of the 1990s and later, here the roof is of a single span, and it is particularly apt being reminiscent of the train shed roofs of Victorian railway stations. The architects have also created a certain anxiety caused by the solid brick walls and central entrance which appear to be held in position by nothing more than margins of black glass.

Texture, colour, wit, comprehensible scale – all have been re-introduced into architecture by buildings like these. But these are lessons that have also been learned by the modernists and incorporated by some into a new wave of modernist building. Examples of neo-modernism can be found in most of our cities. In Bradford it is typified by some of the new offices that have been appearing, but particularly by the suite of retail units and café bars opened (and to be opened) in Centenary Square (6.17). Here cubic form and high rise have been abandoned for a low profile crescent formation that has been clad with sawn stone; but the design remains true to its modernist rootstock in its sleekness and the complete lack of reference to past tradition in detail and its arrangement.

But whether we prefer modernist or postmodernist structures or argue over which is more ideologically suited to the late twentieth and twenty-first centuries, there is one structure that has added greatly to the city's skyline during this period and that is the mosque. Neither modernist nor postmodernist, but of a traditional religious design, the dome and minarets of a mosque like that on Darfield Street (6.18) have made an important impact, yet perhaps hardly noticed, so well do these features blend and complement the historic built environment while also enriching it.

6.19 *Left:* Gateway to the former Mitchell Brothers' Mill, Bowling Lane.

6.20 *Below:* Scaffolding to the entrance of Bradford's Victorian Rawson Market.

6.21 The Kebab Hut, Manningham Lane.

The Ephemeral City

In concluding this exploration of Bradford's architecture it is worth recording some of the structures that architectural historians rarely comment on. The built environment of a city is more than just the sum of its past and present buildings. The built environment has almost a life of its own and one that is composed of buildings in different stages of development. Some stand lifelorn, derelict, a shadow of their former past as buildings; perhaps others have all but disappeared, only a wall, an old outbuilding, a pair of gate piers give any indication of a site once full of activity (6.19). In other parts of the city whole neighbourhoods may become unrecognisable arenas of dirt, chaos and noise as buildings are torn down and the area flattened and redefined. Other structures are rebuilt or restored and while this is happening temporary sculptures are created in the piles of bricks, drainage pipes and other building materials, or in the almost mathematical precision of scaffolding (6.20).

There are also the buildings that were never intended to last, yet they reflect the life of the city just as surely as permanent ones. In the twentieth and twenty-first centuries they are the fast-food stands (6.21) that can be found in any city and particularly where crowds gather. They are also the retail sheds selling anything from tins of beans to underwear. They are relatively cheap to erect, and when trends in retailing change, can easily be disposed of.

It is sites and scenes like these, constantly changing, that are scarcely ever recorded, unless obliquely in the background of other events. And yet they also shape our experience of the built environment and colour our daily perceptions of the life of cities.

FURTHER READING

Histories

Cudworth, William *Histories of Bolton and Bowling* (Bradford, 1891).
– *Histories of Manningham, Heaton and Allerton* (Bradford, 1896).
– *Rambles Round Horton* (Bradford, 1886).
– *Round About Bradford* (Bradford, 1876).

Firth, Gary *Bradford and the Industrial Revolution* (Ryburn Publishing, Halifax, 1990).

James, David *Bradford* (Ryburn Publishing, Halifax, 1990).

Architecture

Ayers, John *Architecture in Bradford* (Bradford Civic Society, 1973).

NOTES

Chapter 1

1. Asa Briggs, *Victorian Cities* (Penguin Books, 1977) p. 157.
2. John James, *The History and Topography of Bradford* (Mountain Press, 1967 (1841)) p. 24.
3. Ibid, pp 64-5.
4. Copies are deposited in Bradford Central Library.
5. Quoted in H.E. Simpson, *A Short History of Bradford Cathedral* (British Publishing Company, 1964) p. 25.
6. We know about this from documents at WYAS Bradford 15D74/1/7/2 and William Scruton *Pen and Pencil Pictures of Old Bradford* (Bradford, 1889) pp 109-10.
7. Mentioned in Surtees Society 92, vol. II, p viii.
8. Joseph Fieldhouse, *Bradford* (Watmoughs Ltd, 1978) pp 61-2.
9. Public Record Office Exchequer Depositions E134/14Chas/Mich 21York.
10. John James, *The History of the Worsted Manufacture in England* (Frank Cass & Co., 1968) (1857)) p. 457.
11. G.W. Conder (ed.) *Memoir and Remains of the Late Revd Jonathan Glyde* (London, 1858) p. 222.
12. John Simpson, *The Journal of Dr John Simpson of Bradford* (Bradford Libraries, 1981) p. 11.
13. G.W. Conder (as at note 10) pp 105, 132.
14. For a fuller account of these events see Jack Reynolds, *The Great Paternalist* (Temple Smith, 1983) pp 105-47.
15. Wright, p. 138.
16. G.W. Conder (as at note 10) pp 342-3.
17. Scruton (as at note 6) preface.
18. Nikolaus Pevsner, *The Buildings of England:Yorkshire West Riding* (Penguin Books, 1959).
19. This correspondence can be followed in the *Telegraph &Argus* and the *Yorkshire Post* during the 1950s and '60s, but particularly the *Yorkshire Post* 19/11/1956, 08/11/1960, 14/08/64; *Telegraph &Argus* 24/10/1967, 25/10/1967.

Chapter 2

1. For a detailed history of these families see William Cudworth, *Histories of Bolton and Bowling* (Bradford, 1891).

Chapter 3

1. WYAS Bradford.
2. William Cudworth, *Rambles Round Horton* (Bradford, 1886) p. 141.

Chapter 4

1. William Cudworth, *Rambles Round Horton* (Bradford, 1886) p. 27.
2. Quoted in Jack Reynolds, *The Great Paternalist* (Maurice Temple Smith, 1983) p. 17.
3. C. Aspin (ed.), *The Yorkshire Textile Districts* in 1849 (Blackburn, 1974) p. 18.
4. Reynolds, *Paternalist*.
5. Quoted in George Ingle, *Yorkshire Cotton* (Carnegie, 1997) p. 113.
6. Frederick Engels, *The Condition of the Working Class in England* (Panther, 1969) p. 74.
7. See Laisterdyke Local History Group, *Remembering Laisterdyke* (Leeds, 1988) pp 2, 30.
8. I am grateful to Paul Jennings of the University of Bradford for this information.

Chapter 5

1. G.W. Conder (ed.), *Memoir and Remains of the late Revd Jonathan Glyde* (London, 1858) p. 343.
2. H. Hodgson, *Fifty Years of Co-operation in Great Horton District* (Manchester, 1909) p. 121.
3. Quoted in Derek Linstrum, *West Yorkshire Architects and Architecture* (Lund Humphries, 1978) p. 280.
4. Quoted in *Education in Bradford since 1870* (Bradford, 1970) p. 217.
5. *The Century's Progress*, 1893 (Scolar Press, 1971) p. 66.
6. Borough of Bradford Reports of Committees of Council 1855-69.
7. West Yorkshire Archive Service, Bradford, Building Plans no. 4404.

Chapter 6

1. James Burnley, *Phases of Bradford Life – In and About Silsbridge Lane* (Bradford, 1870).
2. For a fuller account see Joyce Ashworth, *The Sutton Housing Trust*, T.S. Bradford Central Library, Local Studies.
3. Ralph Tubbs, *Living in Cities*, Penguin, nd, p. 33. Tubbs was one of the architects of the Festival of Britain site.

INDEX

ABOUT THE AUTHOR

Dr George Sheeran works at the University of Bradford in the School of Lifelong Education and Development where he is Associate Dean. He is head of the Pennine and Yorkshire Studies Unit and teaches the regional, architectural and landscape history of Yorkshire. His other publications include:

Landscape Gardens in West Yorkshire 1680-1880, Wakefield Historical Publishing, 1990

Brass Castles: West Yorkshire New Rich and their Houses 1800-1914, Ryeburn/Keele, 1993

Medieval Yorkshire Towns, Edinburgh University Press, 1998